Foundations
for a
New Democracy

Foundations for a New Democracy

Corporate Social Investment in South Africa

How it works,
why it works,
who makes it work,
and how it's making a difference

Myra Alperson

Ravan Press   Johannesburg

Published by Ravan Press
PO Box 145 Randburg 2125
South Africa

First published 1995

ISBN 0 86975 463 7

Cover design: Centre Court Studio
DTP: Rob Irvine

Printed by Creda Press, Cape Town

Contents

PART III
Project profiles 145

Chapter 6
Project profiles

PART III
Beyond CSI 195

Chapter 7
Socially responsible investing: The other side of
    social investment 197

Chapter 8

Ds. C. F. Beyers Naude
Ecumenical Advice Bureau

As all of us in South Africa are facing the challenge of the Reconstruction and Development Programme of our government, it seems to me that five main pillars are needed to build upon the foundation which has been laid during the past few years for a meaningful democracy in South Africa:

1. A truly democratic government which strongly reflects the hopes, ideals and needs of the majority of our people and sincerely wishes to meet those needs where possible.

2. Companies that are concerned with building a foundation as well as a climate for corporate social investment in the new South Africa through the contribution which only such companies can make to the corporate of our country.

3. Trade unions which are willing to promote the interest not only of all workers but also of the whole community.

4. Bodies (especially churches, religious institutions and human rights institutions) with a deep concern for moral and ethical values in business (such as transparency, accountability and a just economic system).

5. Communities with a deep concern for all citizens in their own surroundings, especially for the poor, the less educated, the more disadvantaged and the marginalised.

Chief Rabbi Cyril K. Harris

That the privileged few have to help the underprivileged many, in this country at this time, is not merely a political, economic or social necessity — it is a moral imperative. Hence every avenue of advancement for the masses must be espoused by industry and commerce, including comprehensive job training, improvements to workers' conditions and welfare, and the provision of practical services to workers' families. In addition, firms should be active in supplying subsidies to at least one area of essential social need, be it education, health or security.

The narrowing of the chasm between the First World and the Third World is primarily in the hands of industry. More than any other force or group, big business can help bring about the First World's acceptance of the necessity for accommodation, while simultaneously offering the Third World a level of advancement within its reach.

Joe Slovo, MP (1926-1994)
Minister of Housing

There can be no better time to address the subject of corporate social investment or corporate social responsibility because it undoubtedly has a key role to play in promoting a genuine social commitment by business as the nation undertakes the challenge of the Reconstruction and Development Programme. South African and foreign companies and investors can fulfil a crucial role in helping to build the new democracy during the coming years of transition.

South Africa has the means, the potential skills and the political will to drive a social responsibility Reconstruction and Development Programme. But what we need to do is perhaps to reorder our sense or social priorities. I certainly do not harbour the illusion that business can be driven by pure charity. But there is clearly an area between charity and an approach which is completely dominated by sectional gain. If business does not help to occupy this area, it will be signalling for other solutions.

In the final analysis, corporate social investment, like charity, begins at home. We ourselves — government, the communities and the private sector — will somehow have to put our money where our mouths are. It is unlikely that foreign investors, or those endeavouring to promote the concept of corporate social responsibility, will invest money for this purpose in South Africa before South African institutions have indicated their substantial support and confidence in their own country and the resolution of its problems.

Peter Storey
District Bishop, The Methodist Church of Southern Africa

Without the myriad of social investments by private corporations
around the world, the change process in South Africa would not
have been the same.
Corporate social investment helped us break apartheid — a
similar commitment is now needed to help us build a new nation.

People working in Corporate Social Investment say...

CSI is a form of affirmative action, which means doing "unequal things" to make sure people can be equals.

Hermien Cohn, *Eskom*

You straddle the most interesting mix of people. The real heartbeat comes from seeing people on the ground, especially women. They give me more confidence in the likely success of a project when they're on a committee.

Marc Gonsalves, *JCI*

CSI must be a partnership. People have ideas and vision but they need the resources that we have. They need to be able to see themselves as equal partners with us, and not us as the boss.

Zandile Jakavula, *AECI*

You're making a difference where the need is great.

Michael O'Dowd, *The Anglo American and De Beers Chairman's Fund*

I try to be realistic in my projects. I always think of the company *and* the community; a programme has to work for both.

Mary-Jane Morifi, *BP Southern Africa*

CSI is the most neglected profession. It's not recognised, like public relations or accountants. There's a need to give CSI professionals recognition, along, perhaps, with training and accreditation.

Eunice Sibiya, *Coca-Cola South Africa*

I love my job. It has returned my South Africanness to me and restored parts of my South African identity which were robbed by apartheid.

We [white CSI professionals] have to work ourselves out of a job. I don't see myself here in another three years.

If we don't help NGOs and CBOs become more accountable and transparent, we're not doing our job.

Hilary Ashton, *Nedcor Community Development Fund*

You have to have a social investment heart, a caring attitude for people, not a cold clinical heart. You can teach all the other skills but not how to really care. You need to be dedicated, committed and have a lot of staying power. People get disillusioned if a project isn't finalised within two months. You need to be persistent — it can take a year or two to get off the ground. Then the excitement and satisfaction are extraordinary.

Susan Smit, *Toyota*

Preface

This book came about as the result of reporting I did on corporate social investment (CSI) in South Africa during a four-year span that began in late 1990. Remarkable changes were already under way in how certain forward-thinking companies interpreted their obligations in South Africa's fledgling democracy to promote the economic and social well-being of the communities in which they operate or do business. The best of these companies were already implementing a mini-Reconstruction and Development Programme long before "RDP" became the buzz-letters of South Africa's new society.

As its title states, this book attempts to analyse just how corporate social investment (or, as some firms prefer, "involvement") works, why it works, who makes it work, and how it makes a difference. It does this through profiles of twenty companies chosen for their innovative approach to CSI, followed by shorter profiles of projects these companies have funded. The project profiles are among the CSI managers' favourites, even though they are not necessarily the largest organisations or recipients of the largest grants.

Since the mid-1980s, with a handful starting earlier, a growing number of companies have formed discreet CSI programmes. Some are separate departments or foundations with their own budget and staff to support community projects. Others consist of members of the companies' public affairs or marketing staffs who spend some of their time on CSI.

Some of the programmes are led by individuals and teams with exceptional vision and energy. They have spearheaded innovative CSI projects that have made a major difference in many communities, in some cases kick-starting small new groups which have grown into sophisticated, highly effective service organisations. A few CSI programmes function as quasi-development agencies, sending staff into remote rural areas to assist local development groups, in some cases preferring to provide know-how in lieu of a cheque. And CSI managers increasingly network with each other and collaborate on projects. In 1994, a core number of companies active in CSI, joined by an array of foundations and trusts, formed the Southern Africa Grantmakers' Association (SAGA), a formal network which is sure to grow.

But most companies run lacklustre programmes. While they may agree that paternalism and secrecy have no part in the new South Africa, they have yet to commit themselves to a CSI programme that involves disclosing their social spending budget, promoting employee involvement in CSI or devolving programming to the regional level, or taking risks on high-impact development projects that results in CSI that is more than merely an extension of corporate marketing. A few paragraphs in an annual report, perhaps with a photograph or two, are often the only information (if there's any at all) that anyone outside this elite group will ever see about what the company is doing. Trade unions, in particular, have protested against the heavy-handed approach of companies that exclude them from the CSI process.

For all of corporate South Africa, the time is ripe for an evaluation of new directions and models of corporate social investment. And that's what *Foundations for a New Democracy* aims to do. Through its profiles, it tries to show how companies with vision and courage — and the people behind them — are making CSI an inclusive, developmental process which at its best is a 'win-win' situation for the companies and the constituencies that benefit from their investment.

This is not to say that CSI is a purely do-good effort; far from it. A healthy cynicism is necessary in making the connection between CSI and corporate self-interest, and in perceiving the difference between authentic and superficial CSI. During the review process in which companies had the opportunity to see the profiles in this book and make corrections and updates, some proved to be thin-skinned to criticism and sought alterations to the text that changed their tone. In the end, changes were made to correct errors or update information but not to burnish the corporate image.

* * *

CSI in South Africa should not be studied in isolation. As companies become global, they must examine their role as corporate citizens of the world. A number of South African companies have major operations overseas. Likewise, the American, British, German and Japanese companies that market or make goods in South Africa, or provide services in South Africa, are part of a network of multinational companies operating worldwide.

If a country has a code of conduct banning child labour in one country, does it adhere to the same standard elsewhere? If it practises progressive environmental policies in its home country, are its factories emitting toxic pollutants elsewhere? These are the types of critical questions that must be asked. And a growing number of organisations are asking these questions. So this book provides information in its resource section on some of the groups undertaking research and advocacy on corporate global stewardship.

This is a short book which does not aim to be comprehensive. I'm certain I have overlooked many important topics and projects. And by profiling just a few companies, I've omitted others that are doing excellent work. I trust someone else will take up where I have left off. At the least, I hope this book will serve to kick-start a lively debate on the role that CSI must take in helping to promote a more equitable society in South Africa.

Myra Alperson
Johannesburg 1995

Acknowledgements

The writing of *Foundations for a New Democracy* would not have been possible without funding from The Ford Foundation and The Liberty Life Foundation. Thanks to Dr John Gerhart, Director of Africa Programmes at The Ford Foundation's Johannesburg offices for his very enthusiastic endorsement of the proposal I brought to him in November 1993.

Further funding from The Liberty Life Foundation enabled me to visit projects that the profiled companies support and to complete the book sooner than I had originally planned. In the interest of disclosure (which I discuss in the book), I did not solicit funds from the companies I have profiled, but as editor of *CSI Letter*, a newsletter which chronicled CSI in South Africa, I was in regular contact with CSI managers.

It was over lunch with Hugh McLean at Liberty Life that I described my project and was asked to bring my proposal around. Hylton Appelbaum, the fund's executive director, firmly believes that the dissemination of information plays a key role in promoting a more democratic society, and in backing this book offered helpful (and often witty) insights to the writing process.

The corporate social investment professionals at South Africa's companies — often one-person departments — are among the hardest-working, most creative and busiest people I have met in South Africa. So I also want to thank each one who made time during a particularly hectic period in South Africa — shortly before and after the elections in April 1994 — to see me (sometimes more than once).

I had wonderful, inspiring experiences visiting projects that have benefited from CSI. Thanks to the many people directing these projects whose dedication and imagination shows the great hope for South Africa.

Special thanks to The Conference Board, my employer in New York City, which granted me leave to return to South Africa to complete the book just one month after I had joined its Business and Society research unit. And I must especially thank publisher Glenn Moss at Ravan Press for his willingness to take on this book.

Further thanks must go to the many people who served as advisers, formally and informally, both in South Africa and the US. Their insights, experience and time have made a big difference in my ability to understand the issues and debates surrounding CSI in South Africa. Without their input I do not think I could have done a proper job.

Finally, a very special thanks to Craig Charney for his moral support and many suggestions on how to make the book better.

PART I

CSI in South Africa:
Where it came from and
where it is now

CHAPTER 1

A brief history of CSI in South Africa

Origins

Even though the corporate/community relationship has a rather short history in South Africa, its roots can be traced as far back as the Bible — or so claims British scholar Tom Cannon. In his book *Corporate Responsibility,*[1] he also cites references to it in Chaucer's *Canterbury Tales.*

But the origins of modern Corporate Social Investment (CSI), he writes, stem from the Industrial Revolution, which transformed the way communities were structured and thrust new responsibilities upon employers. Of course, many of them did nothing, or worse — as journalists and novelists of the time wrote in graphic detail. But a few enlightened owners introduced worker welfare funds and supported laws to regulate factory work, oversee health and safety (such as it was in those days), protect chimney sweeps from exploitation and control working conditions for poor children. Victorian paternalism, experiments with co-operatives and self-help "upliftment" programmes, often with religious overtones, followed.

Finally, in the early 20th century, major companies, particularly in the US, took a leading role in funding universities. Supporting education, then as now, was seen to be the best way for companies to repay the communities in which they prospered — and to train a new generation of employees. Cannon uses this background of moderately enlightened self-interest to explain the foundations of modern corporate responsibility in the British and US workplace.

One of the key elements to Cannon's work is his comprehensive definition of corporate responsibility. He goes far beyond community investment to include responsibility in the workplace, toward the environment, in the production and marketing processes *and* the executive boardroom. In short, it's a holistic approach in which

---

[1]Pitman Publishing, 1992, 128 Long Acre, London WC2E 9AN

being a responsible employer applies to every area of corporate conduct.

In South Africa, the history and definition of CSI are far narrower. Many companies, particularly the mining houses, created welfare funds early in their existence, and mining house magnates often sponsored philanthropies in their own name. But these were generally of the most paternalistic kind. And little has been written about them.

CSI in the 1970s: The beginnings

In fact, nothing much had been recorded about corporate involvement in South Africa until 1972, when Meyer Feldberg, then a professor of business at the University of Cape Town (and now dean of the Columbia University Business School in New York City), exhorted business leaders to learn from the model of their US counterparts to get involved in the communities in which they operated, sold products or drew employees.[2] His reasoning was based on common sense: "I believe that to *subordinate* profits to broad social goals would be totally irresponsible," he said. "On the other hand, socially responsible behaviour is essential to the long-term growth and profitability of the corporation. The costs of carrying out social responsibilities should be considered *as normal costs of doing business"* [italics author's].

Until the late 1960s, US companies had had a long but relatively unremarkable history of CSI. A few firms, such as IBM, introduced pioneering in-house and community programmes early in their own history. But this was the exception. However, massive racial unrest in many American inner cities in the 1960s, coupled with Lyndon Johnson's vision of a Great Society — a precursor, perhaps, to South Africa's Reconstruction and Development Programme (RDP) — prompted corporate America to examine how to take a proactive role in alleviating poverty.

In Detroit, site of some of the era's worst riots, General Motors and other companies established new programmes to reinvigorate devastated neighbourhoods through investment in small business development, bursaries and community upliftment programmes. Employees were encouraged to donate volunteer time to local projects. And, pressurised by shareholders and national "watchdog" groups, GM began publishing a Public Interest Report — now an

---

[2]C. Charney, "Community Action is a Growth Industry", *Management,* April 1993. See also "Business Profits and Social Responsibility", University of Cape Town, Inaugural Lecture, New Series No. 10, 15 June 1972.

annual supplement to its business report — which describes not only its community programmes but also its achievements in recruiting, training and promoting blacks, women and people from other disadvantaged groups into skilled and management jobs, and new energy-saving initiatives to protect the environment.

Meyer Feldberg's talk was just the first of a few milestones in South African CSI in the 1970s. The next was the creation of the Anglo American and De Beers Chairman's Fund in 1973, and, after that, the formation of the Urban Foundation in 1976 as a private sector initiative to address critical urban development issues in volatile townships nationwide.

Even then, most CSI programmes (which weren't yet called CSI) were generally *ad hoc* donations programmes. Little attention was given to develop a strict definition of CSI, to monitor the projects that were being funded and to examine creative partnerships between business and its stakeholders that could make such investment go further. Simply put, there was no public demand for it; during the age of apartheid, when information was carefully controlled — and, more often, withheld — the disclosure of such information was not yet part of the debate.

The Sullivan Principles and US companies: A turning point

In 1977, the creation of the Sullivan Principles applying to US companies (and corresponding guidelines for firms operating within the European Community) established a new vocabulary for CSI in South Africa. (The term more frequently used by the code's signatory companies was corporate social responsibility.) US companies operating in South Africa voluntarily complied with the Principles, but constant scrutiny by shareholders and anti-apartheid activists back home made the "voluntariness" almost moot.

Institutional investors, particularly from religious organisations, municipal pension funds and trade unions, pressurised companies either to disclose in great detail the extent of their social investment in South Africa — or to close up shop. They were exhorted to stop supplying the South African military or to make loans to the government. Whether the companies liked the Principles or not — and many signatory companies didn't — as a result of agreeing to abide by them many developed creative, proactive CSI programmes that included extensive community investment as well as spending on employee wellbeing. Under Sullivan, CSI covered such employee concerns as housing, health and training to enable employees to advance on the job, and education of family members.

An audit of signatory compliance to the Principles, conducted by a private consulting firm, was a time-consuming and exacting process. A number of companies hired outside consultants to write up their reports for submission — a new form of job creation generated by Sullivan!

First efforts at CSI networking

While US-owned companies haggled with the Sullivan Code, a number of South African owned companies, around the mid-1980s, formed charitable trusts, both to accommodate expanded community investment and to get tax relief for certain types of it — mainly donations to tertiary institutions.

The idea and scope of CSI began changing by the mid-1980s. Companies began talking to each other, to share their woes and their ideas. An effort at creating a formal CSI network, instigated in 1988 by Kobus Visagie, who had just taken over the Gencor Development Trust, foundered. One CSI manager who recalls this experience attributes its demise to the preference by companies in those days to go it alone so that they could get full credit on projects they funded. But a few dozen CSI managers, including Visagie, continued to meet on a regular, though informal, basis, to brainstorm on policy and development trends.

Turning trends into practice

In 1990, the Liberty Life Foundation, whose executive director took part in this informal network, invited companies to join in a national educare initiative. (Investment in early childhood educare is not tax-deductible in South Africa.) This effort may have been too soon or too bold. When no one came calling, the Foundation pledged R100 million over five years for educare investment.

One year later, 15 companies (including, among those profiled in this book, Anglo American, Gencor, JCI, Shell, Southern Life and Standard Bank) joined forces with a spectrum of political parties, trade unions and black advocacy groups — and pledged R500 million to launch the Joint Education Trust (JET). JET was formed as a five-year national "kick-start" programme to support existing programmes with successful projects in three areas: (1) upgrading the quality of teaching in the formal education system; (2) advancing literacy and numeracy for adults with the most basic education needs; and (3) improving education and job prospects for unemployed youth no longer in school.

The funds for JET were in addition to pre-set CSI budgets. This type of commitment symbolised the new pressures on companies, similar to the demands of the RDP, to put their money where their mouths were.

New trends in the 1990s

The JET initiative is just one example of the process through which companies began to take a more proactive and co-operative role in the social change process, in which the Consultative Business Movement (CBM), established in 1988, was a leader. Following the reforms that began officially in February 1990 (but were already unofficially under way for quite some time), South African CSI began to open up significantly. This process was spurred by a number of developments:

■ The discussions about a new democracy in South Africa had, inevitably, to be applied to the way South African companies function. Organisations like CBM played a key role in facilitating these talks;

■ More forward-thinking companies, recognising that democracy is an inclusive process, began to decentralise their CSI programmes, moving away from the chairman's office into public affairs, human resources or self-contained departments. In some instances, CSI was devolved into regional operations, where management and employees understood local community needs. Several "chairman's funds" were renamed Community Development Funds to reflect the greater connection to grassroots groups and the fact that policy decisions on corporate donations were no longer a one-way process emanating from the top;

■ Companies published more information about their spending. While by no means an across-the-board trend, certain firms were producing social reports that were not just glossy depictions of funded projects but also listed grant recipients, how much they received, and the thinking that had gone on to set CSI policy and choose projects. However, very few reports went into extensive detail;

■ Articles about CSI began to appear more widely in the mainstream press. While some were public relations pronouncements trumpeting projects that companies had just funded, others were critical examinations of the role of CSI in South Africa's development process. In 1991, the *Weekly Mail & Guardian* launched what has become an annual "Investing in the Future" supplement to analyse trends in CSI. This supplement was accompanied by an award honouring South Africa's "Most Caring Companies". *People Dynamics* magazine, the publication of the Institute for Personnel Management, published occasional articles on the subject. *The Innes Labour Brief*, which targets industrial relations and human resources managers, ran articles on this topic and also published *CSI Letter*, South Africa's only national newsletter on CSI. (The author of this book was founding editor of *CSI Letter* and has written articles on CSI for *The Innes Labour Brief*.) *Finance Week* magazine ran a series of corporate profiles that included a "scorecard" rating the companies' CSI programmes;

- Starting in the late 1980s, Business & Marketing Intelligence, a for-profit business research company, launched surveys on social investment spending through a biennial "Corporate Care Check". Some of this research, now carried out by an independent consultant formerly associated with BMI, is confidential and "owned" by the clients who commission it, so that useful information is withheld from public debate;

- An increasing number of conferences and workshops were run to explore new issues in CSI. These were initially low-key, low-cost meetings which reflected the relatively low status of CSI personnel in a company. But in mid-1994, an expensive two-day CSI conference attracted about 120 participants to discuss topics such as the input of trade unions in CSI, the possible implications of new tax policy and how small companies may operate effective CSI programmes. (Critics said the money should have been used on CSI and wondered if the company sponsoring the conference had any CSI of its own.)

- On their own, companies began networking with each other to share resources on individual projects or to link up in particular regions. These networks proved particularly useful for small regional companies with minimal capacity for in-house CSI. The Social Involvement Association in the Western Cape was the prototype for this type of initiative. With a membership of 200, it sponsors regular meetings, publishes a quarterly newsletter and helped organise the Corporate Action Network (CAN) of local companies, including some very small ones, to share work on a job-creation initiative in Khayelitsha township. A Gauteng counterpart to CAN was also created. Some CAN members come from corporate marketing departments, representing a trend in which CSI is linked with line business functions;

- US firms in South Africa, no longer constrained by the Signatory

Association on how to run their CSI programmes — and how much they had to spend to get a top rating — planned to form a subcommittee within the American Chamber of Commerce to continue the networking that they had found so valuable;

- Other foreign firms in South Africa are examining how they can best contribute to South Africa's redevelopment — and link it to solid business practices. The Prince of Wales Business Leaders Forum, seeing South Africa as the gateway to investment in sub-Saharan Africa, sponsored a forum bringing British-owned businesses together with key South African non-government organisations (NGOs) to discuss how they could implement worthwhile business/community programmes. (A number of non-British firms, including American Express, BMW and Volkswagen, belong to the Forum and help sponsor its activities.)

- And CSI has been increasingly linked to the RDP as a means to focus private sector spending which the government has said is essential if the RDP is to succeed. In fact, some CSI professionals claim that what they have been doing all along *is* RDP, although this sentiment is not unanimous. BMI Issues Management has embarked on a project to develop an evaluation mechanism to see how companies comply with the RDP with respect to their support for NGOs. This process can perhaps be seen as the local counterpart to the Statement of Principles in that it would create a uniform framework to measure corporate social performance.

A new SAGA:
Economic pressures bring people together

During this period, economic pressures on CSI departments, as well as the expectation that a new government would ask companies to contribute more funding for national redevelopment, prompted renewed discussions about the merits of a formal donor network. This time local foundations and trusts as well as foreign donors working in South Africa were invited to join. In October 1993, a core group of delegates from 30 companies and other donor groups met in Broederstroom to map out the preliminary framework for such a network.

The following January, several hundred companies were then invited to Nasrec, the Johannesburg conference centre, for a day-long "brainstorming" session, in a large group and smaller working groups, to take the discussions further. This was to include the naming of the organisation and the election of a steering committee to develop proposals for a constitution, a structure and a preliminary budget. About 85 corporate and private donors were represented. By the end of the day, a steering committee had been formed to draft a planning document for what was to be called the Southern Africa Grantmakers Association, or SAGA.

The working paper that emerged covered a number of key areas for CSI networking. One was the importance of communication and information: co-ordinating a process of information sharing through conferences, a database and publications, on projects, accountability and enhancing the professional capacity of CSI professionals and other donors. Such information could include a calendar of events; information on legislation and public policies affecting donors; enhancing the skills of being a grantmaker and evaluating projects; promoting the overall role of CSI within the corporation and in wider society; interacting with other groups beyond the donor network; and exploring the different roles donors might take in the RDP.

SAGA was formally launched at the Carlton Hotel on 3 August 1994. About 60 companies and other funders, including the Kagiso Trust, Interfund, the Ford Foundation and the Charles Stewart Mott Foundation, were present.

But even then, questions remained about the value of such a network, drawing on past concerns about problems in "sharing" projects, as well as the possibility that a funding "cartel" might emerge. A number of key companies that had been present at the January meeting were absent at the August launch. Critics of SAGA complained that the sliding membership fee based on the size of CSI budgets, but allocating only one vote per member, was a form of taxation without representation. And they objected to the creation of a new structure that would consume funds that could otherwise be channelled directly into CSI.

But the pluses outweighed the minuses — especially at a time when CSI professionals were feeling a bit "under siege" by the prospect that government spending on the RDP might replace their function. It turned out, however, that government welcomed increased CSI. Working together, both to professionalise and broaden the profile of CSI, made the concept of SAGA an appealing one, and an interim board of directors was elected to take SAGA to its first full general meeting in early 1995. An executive director, Elaine Davie, was named in May 1995.

With the launch of SAGA — despite the dissenters — CSI had

come almost full circle in South Africa. Meyer Feldberg's call more than two decades before had been acknowledged. And South African companies, now clearly better connected to the communities in which they work, have taken the lead in creating innovative CSI programmes that make a difference — and can serve as a models for CSI elsewhere in the developing world.

CHAPTER 2

How CSI works in South Africa
(based on the companies profiled in this book)

Structure

There is no single formula or format to cover the operation of all the South African CSI departments profiled in this book. A few companies fund autonomous foundations with their own board of directors, while others incorporate CSI into public affairs, group communications, and, sometimes, their marketing departments. Some foundations draw their trustees from top corporate management or from member companies, as in the case of the Gencor Development Trust. In others, such as the Southern Life Foundation, some trustees are recruited from communities which the foundations serve.

In a few cases, the CSI departments function semi-independently within the company, as one- or two-person operations answerable principally to the chief executive. In the exceptional situation of the Premier Group, CSI is coordinated by the Human Resources Department but most funding decisions are made by social investment councils made up of equal numbers of workers (mainly trade union members) and managers. In 1993 AECI introduced regional mechanisms involving workers and managers for project evaluation.

Smaller companies often have an entirely different situation: a lone person administering some CSI, or no official CSI programme at all. These companies often complain that they don't have enough staff and cannot administer projects properly or process the appeals that come in. For this reason, consortia such as the Corporate Action Network (with branches in Gauteng and the Western Cape), the Social Involvement Association of the Western Cape, the Boksburg Industrialists' Association and other regional groups and SAGA, offer opportunities for smaller companies to find project partners.

Budgets are generally allocated from a percentage of pre-tax or after-tax profits, although some companies designate a percentage of dividends for CSI spending. Budgets for tertiary education support often come from separate accounts and are frequently administered separately as well. (These are often described as cheque-writing procedures that do not need the expertise of a CSI manager.)

The figure that most frequently cropped up in this research among companies willing to disclose their social spending is 1 to 1,5 percent of post-tax profits. Murray & Roberts places 5 percent of its ordinary dividend into its foundation for social investment; the Anglo American and De Beers' Chairman's Fund and the Gencor Development Trust also draw on dividends.

A number of companies have chosen themes as a way to focus their social spending. The Colgate-Palmolive South Africa Foundation, in line with an international campaign spearheaded by its New York-based corporate parent, emphasises multicultural youth programmes. Pick 'n Pay has made its mark as South Africa's "green" company, particularly supporting environmental initiatives; this campaign is closely linked to the marketing of Pick 'n Pay "green" products. Eskom, not surprisingly, emphasises electrification, with an explicit focus on helping to electrify small businesses and schools. Gencor has explored ways to recycle former mining properties for community investment purposes, including schools and training centres. Liberty Life has given high priority to early childhood educare. In addition to larger projects, most companies allocate a portion of their CSI budget for donations to general welfare organisations, picking up some of the slack from state budget cuts.

Employee involvement is still limited. The most proactive example among companies profiled in this book is the Social Investment Council system at Premier Group in which equal numbers of management and employees, most of them members of the largest union represented at the company, make decisions on regional giving. One company in this study, Liberty Life, has introduced a matching grants programme through which the foundation equals employees' charitable contributions with gifts ranging from R25 to R2 000 to eligible organisations.

Several other companies have employee committees that have some input on CSI. BMW's Early Childcare Centre arose as an employee initiative and draws support from an employee-run raffle. British Petroleum South Africa (BPSA), whose CSI is under new leadership, has created a database of employee skills in order to match employee-volunteers with community organisations that could benefit from their expertise.

Companies that were signatories to the Statement of Principles were required to get employees involved in community projects to earn the highest rating. "Adopt-a-School" programmes were popular examples, and some companies will continue with these. Warner-Lambert has supported networking among small companies in the Western Cape and was a founder of the Social Involvement Association which has promoted project collaboration and sponsored township tours.

In conjunction with the RDP, many companies are linking their CSI to explicit projects in skills training and job creation. At the time this book was being prepared, a number of companies were discussing how they might link up CSI programmes to the RDP. JCI indicated that top corporate executives make regular consultations with its CSI managers on public policy concerns. The Nedcor Community Development Fund was incorporated into a new unit that addresses the needs of the RDP. Shell and BMW are adapting their CSI strategies to address RDP goals. By publication date, many more will surely have joined in.

As CSI-RDP linkages increase, so will monitoring of their work. It is this author's belief that despite the scrapping of the Statement of Principles to which US companies in South Africa voluntarily agreed during the sanctions era, a new monitoring system may evolve into a uniform code of conduct applying to all companies. (Most companies hate the term "code of conduct", so another will probably be devised.) Following RDP criteria, some of which resemble those of the Statement of Principles, companies will be expected to make ongoing financial and in-kind contributions to South African redevelopment. Proactive companies will publicise their social investment activities.

How funding applications are screened

It is typical for a CSI administrator to complain about the pile of proposals he or she receives daily. South Africa's NGOs have become sophisticated and aggressive about approaching funders for support. The better-equipped NGOs prepare fancy fundraising proposals, sometimes assisted by a consultant. They may then send proposals to all listed companies on the Johannesburg Stock Exchange, so that one CSI manager might receive several copies of the same proposal that we sent to company subsidiaries because they are all ultimately directed to his or her office.

Grassroots groups that lack this capacity may submit handwritten proposals. A number of firms have developed formal application forms in order to assure that they can make decisions based on well-structured proposals with complete budgets. But so as not to exclude worthwhile NGOs that lack the wherewithal to complete the application forms, some companies sometimes offer assistance. Among companies profiled in this study, Anglo American, Liberty Life and Nedcor indicated that they can provide such help. Other CSI programmes, such as the Standard Bank Foundation, said that they will not consider any proposal that is not submitted on its standard form. Gencor Development Trust expressed a preference to give fewer but larger grants to groups that have a lot of capacity. Limited staffing and time constraints are among the reasons cited for not being more proactive in the applications-screening process.

One drawback of this latter policy is that worthwhile small organisations may be automatically excluded from consideration. At this writing, partly in response to concerns about how the government will allocate RDP funds, many NGOs were in the process of forming common-interest NGO forums or associations to apply for funding as a group. One example of an existing forum is AIDSLink, which brings together several dozen small organisations involved in a wide range of educational and support projects related to AIDS, and enables them to raise money under one umbrella.

Grant decisions vary with the company criteria and policies, which are described in the profiles that follow. Small grants may sometimes be selected by the CSI official alone or as others draw on the recommendations of grants committees, and large grants are generally be submitted to a committee of top executives for their approval.

Monitoring donations

Some companies do little follow-up once donations are given; JCI and Pick 'n Pay admitted that they rarely have the time or capacity for such follow-up. Other firms require regular report-backs on a quarterly, semi-yearly or annual basis. This helps them evaluate the worthiness of the project, although some of the recipient groups object that filing these reports takes up time they would rather invest in projects. (The NGO that was most vocal about this is a well-established organisation with a policy of full disclosure. Its executive director feels that such report-backs are redundant.)

Another way to monitor donations is to make a grant but allot funds as they are needed. The Liberty Life Foundation requires its grantees to file monthly grant requests which include a budget on how the funding will be used. The Foundation has the staffing capacity to handle this paperwork, but this is not the case with most CSI departments.

CSI disclosure

There are no disclosure laws in South Africa governing CSI spending (unless it is done through a separate trust) and many companies won't say how much they allocate or spend and precisely who receives funds. Some corporate annual reports reserve a few paragraphs or some pages for CSI, but often the material is summarised in such a general fashion that little useful information is revealed.

There are healthy trends to indicate that this vagueness and secrecy are going the way of the old South Africa. Some companies now publish separate social investment reports. These range from glossy publications that provide little more than pictures with captions describing a handful of funded projects to detailed social reports. Among companies profiled in this book, the most thorough social reports came from Liberty Life, Pick 'n Pay and the Toyota South Africa Foundation.

Other companies include some social information in their annual reports, among them Anglo American, Murray & Roberts and the Premier Group. Nedcor and Standard Bank indicate that future social reports will include more spending information. BPSA publishes an easy-to-read guide on how CSI works that enables all employees to have access to the process.

CSI networks

CSI is increasingly becoming a collaborative process, both informally and, with the formation of SAGA (see chapter 1), a more structured undertaking. Networking provides a number of benefits, including information on worthwhile new projects and contacts with grassroots community groups doing exceptionally good work. And, as mentioned in some of the profiles, companies draw on their specific strengths for certain projects and can then consult colleagues to make contributions in the areas which they can cover very well. JCI, which has maintained a low profile in CSI, has been known to help "top off" projects with extra funding for which it may not get credit. The company is rethinking its strategy and may develop a more proactive, visible approach.

Trade union attitudes towards CSI

Trade unions have traditionally been hostile towards CSI policymakers, and some companies, likewise, do not solicit trade union input on their CSI. But there are signs of change. Drawing on the model of Premier's Social Investment Councils, there has been some pressure to bring trade union members on to project selection committees. This is already happening on a limited basis. Gencor's Employee-Community Support Groups enlist union members to identify worthwhile projects to fund and then to draw up funding proposals. Likewise, Murray & Roberts plans to decentralise some of its CSI and to encourage employees to get involved. The Toyota South Africa Foundation has appointed a former shop steward to take the full-time job of projects assistant in the CSI unit. He was offered this position after he had already spent considerable time assisting with project identification and oversight. But he will be put on a career path that will eventually bring him into a corporate line position.

The benefit of such involvement is obvious: when employees, whether or not they are union members, become part of the CSI process, they can claim a certain understanding and even ownership of projects. This input not only draws on their own knowledge of the communities that the companies want to help but also endows them with responsibility to ensure that CSI monies are used appropriately and the programmes succeed. Such accountability can only follow, however, in an atmosphere of complete openness, because involvement without transparency can lead to abuse of the job.

The Community Growth Fund (CGF), a union-owned unit trust formed in 1992, has pushed this process along. By seeking to choose companies for inclusion in its investment portfolio based on work-place practices and other social concerns directly related to worker well-being, CGF has highlighted the important relationship between good business practices and profits. Similarly, its periodic reports on decisions to exclude companies, and why, has prompted some of these companies to change their policies. And its strong performance since its launch has underscored the role that responsible — and responsive — corporate stewardship can play in building a more equitable society (see also chapter 7).

PART II

CSI Programme Profiles

CHAPTER 3

How the companies were chosen and how the profiles were developed

Choosing the companies

The purpose of this book is to illustrate the scope of CSI being practiced in South Africa. Twenty companies of different sizes and a variety of industries are included.

Those profiled were chosen for their representative importance or innovation and their willingness to cooperate with this study. The **Anglo American and De Beers Chairman's Fund** had to be included because it is the largest corporate donor in South Africa, has the oldest established fund and has had enormous influence in CSI policy-making.

Others were chosen because of their originality.

The **Premier Group** was among the first South African companies to create social investment councils that have equal management and employee representation in decision-making.

Pick 'n Pay unabashedly links its CSI with marketing by administering it through the marketing department, but publishes one of South Africa's most thorough social reports. (Other companies claim to keep their CSI programmes as removed from marketing as possible.)

Toyota South Africa was profiled because of its unusual extent of disclosure, the degree of employee involvement in communities and the linkage of community involvement with job appraisals.

The **Southern Life Foundation** has found ways to make a small budget go far by helping to launch good programmes that other donors might find risky. In some cases, Southern then "exits" from the programme while others add support, or it helps an organisation on another project.

A number of companies were selected because they are foreign-owned and their CSI draws in small or large part on overseas models. **The Colgate-Palmolive Foundation, The Lotus Trust** and

Warner-Lambert are linked to their US parents. Colgate-Palmolive and Warner-Lambert, which remained in South Africa throughout the sanctions period, drew on the Sullivan Code and its successor, the Statement of Principles, to structure their CSI.

Each is taking a different approach to CSI now that sanctions have been scrapped: Colgate-Palmolive is maintaining a high spending level and adhering to themes developed by its parent company; Warner-Lambert, which has been very active in Western Cape networking, will reduce its budget and realign its programme to be closer to business needs. **Lotus,** a recent returnee to South Africa, has a small but very targeted, proactive CSI programme which draws in part on international philanthropy guidelines set by the parent.

Coca-Cola South Africa, when it was known as National Beverage Service, spun off from its disinvesting parent, Coca-Cola, and created a very different form of CSI. Now that it has been re-purchased, it will be interesting to see how or if the essential CSI orientation changes. At the time of publication, its staff had increased from two to four.

BMW also has a foreign parent, but its CSI is rooted in local concerns rather than German models. The company has chosen to take an inward, employee-focused approach, and concentrates most of its CSI on one project, the BMW Childcare Centre, whose operation empowers employees and gives their children a quality headstart in education.

Shell South Africa, which is 60 percent Dutch-owned and 40 percent British-owned, played a major, highly visible role in bolstering human rights efforts in the face of boycott threats from the international anti-apartheid movement. It was thus essential to examine its current CSI programming, to find out how its CSI has changed in the 'new' South Africa.

British Petroleum South Africa (BPSA) is a wholly-owned subsidiary of a British firm, but its very original CSI programme is largely shaped by the personality and ideas of Mary-Jane Morifi, who took the reins only in October 1993.

Some companies profiled are *not* at this time particularly innovative. **Murray & Roberts** does not now conduct an especially original form of CSI, but was chosen because it is a large, influential company that uses a sophisticated communication programme to promote its image. However, the company took a risk in linking CSI with the profit motive when it created creating a for-profit company, Sunflower Projects, to provide job skills and entrepreneurship training. The structure did not work out, but Murray & Roberts remained committed to the concept, 'bailed out' the company and turned it into a not-for-profit operation.

Some companies use their CSI as quasi-development agencies: examples include **Eskom, the Gencor Development Trust, JCI** and **the Nedcor Community Development Fund**. These companies also link hands in partnership with each other to make programmes more effective. The **Liberty Life Foundation**, which has quickly grown into what is believed to be South Africa's second largest corporate donor, also does a lot of hands-on development, but with an explicit emphasis on supporting educare facilities and other areas of 'social transformation'.

AECI runs what it calls a Quality of Life Budget which is increasingly engaging employee involvement. In addition, it 'adds value' to its funding by helping to build capacity among NGOs by "loaning" the expertise of its in-house industrial relations staff.

And the **Standard Bank Foundation** was included because of its size, its concerted decision to raise its public profile, the synergy under way between the Foundation and its human resources and marketing operations, and the way in which it is democratising the grant-making process.

Preparing the research

The CSI administrators at about 30 companies were contacted by letter with a request for an interview and description of the project. The letter also contained a list of 15 questions for discussion purposes. There was no written questionnaire to be filled in; the aim was to arrange a long personal interview that would use the questions as guidelines.

In some cases, the interviews included other people. The Premier profile draws on two interviews: an earlier one I held with a number of key people from the social investment councils and a later meeting with Diane McGurk. At Gencor, JCI, Liberty Life, Nedcor and Shell I met with two or more people.

Most interviews lasted about an hour and a half, but a few went more quickly and others lasted for more than two hours or required further visits. Each interviewee was assured that he or she would see a draft profile for correction and updating purposes. Only one company that was approached agreed to participate and then refused to be interviewed: South African Breweries: Beer Division. This was quite surprising since the company has a very positive reputation for its CSI. Other companies either did not respond to the initial letter or were not contacted a second time.

The questions were as follows:

1 How do you/does your company define CSI? (Or do you prefer a different term?)
2 Can you describe how CSI was developed at the company?
3 Do you operate within a separate department or is CSI administered by marketing, public affairs, human resources, etc.?
   3a How many staff do you have?
4 How much did the company spend in the 1993 financial year? How is the sum determined?
5 Do you publish information on CSI spending? If yes, where?
6 What are the company's spending priorities?
   6a How are these determined?
7 Can you name the five largest recipients of CSI funds from the company?
   7a How were these selected?
   7b Do the recipients approach you for funds? If yes, how?
8 How do you monitor the recipients?
   8a Have there been major failures? How do you identify them? What do you do about them? What have you learned from them?
   8b What were your major successes? Why? Have you been able to replicate them?
9 Are employees involved in CSI? If yes, how? Has employee involvement been successful? How does your company inform employees about CSI activities?
10 Are trade unions involved in CSI decision-making or policy?
11 Are local communities involved in CSI programming? If yes, how?
12 How did you get into doing CSI? What is your background? What qualities do you think a good CSI administrator needs? Do you believe blacks should run CSI departments? Are there blacks in your department? Has your job become easier or harder in recent years? Do you love your job? Do you ever reach burnout? What do you do about it?
13 How is CSI changing? Do you network with your counterparts at other companies? If yes, how?
14 Is there anything in terms of programming or administration that your company has done which is unique? If so, what is it?
15 Are you optimistic about the current trends in CSI?

    A sixteenth question was added after the initial list was prepared. It asked the administrator to identify a favourite project that the company had funded. This project did not have to be one that had received a lot of money but, preferably, was unusual in its approach and/or had been particularly successful. It was often interesting to hear about projects that had received limited funds but had grown over time. I tried to visit as many of the projects as possible to see how corporate support had enabled them to carry on.

Limitations

Foundations for a New Democracy is a short book meant to provide insights into CSI that have not been assembled in one place before. It also aims to offer a platform for debate and discussion about CSI. It generally lacks worker insights into CSI as well as a broader perspective on this topic. These important concerns can, and should, be covered in a future publication.

In the past, South Africa's trade unions have criticised CSI as a way for companies to exert influence in the communities in which they operate — and to generate publicity — without passing profits or the use of them directly to the workforce. As more companies begin to approach their workforce about CSI involvement and create genuine partnerships with their unionised and non-union employees, this criticism may level off.

Profiling just 20 companies omits many others whose CSI programmes are very interesting. No black-owned companies are included. Although some very small companies have been profiled, most lack the resources to invest in a highly developed CSI programme. The example of Warner-Lambert's networking with other companies in the Western Cape should encourage smaller firms to find ways to join other companies or to develop a CSI "theme" that enables them to focus limited resources on specific projects.

Accountability to the profiled companies

All companies profiled had the opportunity to review drafts of the profiles for factual review and updates. Their corrections and many of their comments have been incorporated into the accounts that appear in this book, but I have omitted those suggestions that clearly aimed to burnish the corporate image or water down criticisms of the company.

CHAPTER 4

Overall findings

Although each of the companies profiled has a different tradition, ethos and goals, some common features and trends can be found in almost all of the CSI programmes. This chapter summarises these, for example:

In policy terms

- CSI is being increasingly linked to the government's RDP. Some CSI managers are consulted to help make public policy inputs and some CSI departments are being deliberately restructured to take the RDP into account;
- More companies are willing to disclose information on CSI policy, budgeting, actual spending and the names of recipients, in separate CSI reports or in the corporate annual report. Although such disclosure is limited, it indicates an awareness of a more positive public perception of companies that make an effort to be more truly transparent. It also reflects the understanding that transparency is inherent in a democratic society;
- In some cases, CSI programmes are reaching out to increase support to black-run grassroots organisations rather than through white-run intermediaries, with a particular thrust toward rural NGOs. However, in other instances, the CSI programmes prefer funding such "capacity-building" intermediary NGOs as the Get Ahead Foundation and the Triple Trust Organisation, which have developed a sound structure and a track record in service delivery. In all cases, the goal is to reach more directly to the grassroots and to empower communities that have missed out on other opportunities;
- More employee input is being sought, though still on a limited basis, through participation on selection committees or evaluating projects.

In practice

- Some CSI managers are pushing to have their job or department recognised as a key business function within the company, sometimes tying the position into line management and giving it a career path;

- Some larger companies with nationwide operations are decentralising their CSI programmes, in order to encourage more involvement by employees who are normally *not* directly involved in CSI. The Standard Bank Foundation allocates a CSI budget to each of its six regional divisions; Premier Group's Social Investment Councils operate in eight regions; AECI has regionalised its CSI; and Eskom has community development experts in its generating stations and regional offices;

- Employee newsletters and other company publications contain more information on CSI so that employees know what is going on. In some cases they are encouraged to become involved and are recognised for it. One corporate foundation, Liberty Life Foundation, has launched a matching fund programme based on a US model through which the company equals an employee's donation to an accredited non-profit organisation;

- Some companies have increased their consultation (and, in some cases, interaction) on CSI with trade unions, but this is still a limited process, and difficult to implement — and some firms remain hostile to the idea;

- Companies are demanding more accountability from grantees and linking their donations more closely to business needs. This appears to be the case with certain US-owned companies no longer constrained by the Sullivan Principles and their successor, the Statement of Principles, which sometimes required them to engage in community projects which had no connection whatever to the company's business needs;

- Many more companies are collaborating on CSI projects. Where companies once felt that by joining hands on a project they might lose the visibility that they could promote as a sole sponsor, many now acknowledge that working cooperatively brings more benefit to the receiving organisation. In arranging these partnerships, the companies often take on different tasks, depending on their strengths. There's a much greater understanding of how working together can make a project more successful — and distribute the accountability and liability;

- The practice of CSI is both easier and harder these days, report CSI practitioners. It's easier because the NGOs seeking support tend to be more sophisticated in their applications for funds. And it's harder, in some respects, for the very same reasons: there are many more capable groups competing for a finite amount of funding. Almost all CSI managers interviewed report that they are swamped with applications and that the quality of the applications has improved markedly — some to the point of being slick;

■ CSI positions fall increasingly into the affirmative action category, and a number of whites currently holding these jobs expect their successors to be black; in some cases, they are already mentoring black candidates for their own positions. A number of CSI practitioners listed specific reasons why blacks *should* run the programmes, but they also had reasons why blacks should *not* run them, saying that some black CSI managers might find themselves caught between loyalties on which group to fund. There was also some cynicism about using CSI as an affirmative action post that might be given to an individual who functions as 'little more than a "messenger" for white managers. There was a general acceptance of a healthy synergy between white and black CSI managers, but a preference for black managers who can go into the field and speak the languages of the communities they are working with;

■ CSI is becoming a much more hands-on practice, as managers try to make a growing number of visits into the field to see projects at work. These visits help assure accountability of how CSI money is spent;

■ The application and monitoring processes are more structured, with many companies requiring grantees to file regular reports;

■ More efforts are being made to identify good black-run projects, particularly in rural areas, that provide direct services to needy communities. This form of project selection contrasts markedly with earlier patterns, when there were few good black-run groups to choose from and organisations like the Urban Foundation could rely on regular support from the corporate funders who launched it. The Urban Foundation merged with Consultative Business Movement (CBM) in late 1994 to form the National Business Initiative.

What's still missing
■ **The idea that CSI should also apply to internal workforce policies is absent from most corporate CSI policies in South Africa.** A few companies do link the running of CSI to internal

operations, including human resources and environmental stewardship. Pick 'n Pay's social reports contain information on programmes for employees. The Standard Bank Foundation recognises a healthy synergy between community investment and employee well-being, and expects interactions between human resources and the foundation to grow. But for many firms, the 'C in CSI is tied more to the word "community" than to "company", and excludes employee concerns.

It is possible that some of the workplace unrest that occurred in 1994 after the April election could be linked to this exclusion. Perhaps, as at companies like BMW, tying CSI to internal workplace concerns would give employees a greater sense of ownership and lend itself to a more cooperative (and not co-optive!) atmosphere;

■ **Full accountability.** Once a grant is given, some companies never keep track of what happens to it. While the processing of applications, interviews and project visits is very time-consuming, so is the all-important follow-up process to ensure that recipients are doing what they claim. A few of the companies are surprisingly weak in this area.

By the same token, CSI programmes themselves are not currently fully accountable to stakeholders. As discussed below, a more transparent, participatory CSI would address this shortcoming;

■ **General transparency.** Although there is a trend to disclose more information, CSI is still for the most part treated as a public relations exercise to bolster a company's public image. Most of the social reports now published lack a thorough explanation of how CSI works, how much money companies spend on it, who makes the decisions about it, and how the receiving groups work with the company;

■ **Access to CSI information and programming on the part of employees, particularly trade unions.** Little is done to explain the CSI process or to inform employees about CSI at their company. This is changing at some companies, as in-house newsletters include some details on CSI projects. An excellent example is *Foundation Focus*, a quarterly in-house newsletter of the Southern Foundation which explains the types of projects being funded. Eskom has funded the publication of books to help community-based organisations, particularly in rural areas, get a better understanding of how to apply for funding. As part of its Social Investment Councils programme, Premier offers courses in

basic financial literacy so that employees on the councils understand how to read corporate financial reports. And BPSA publishes an easy-to-read guide to CSI for employees.

CHAPTER 5

Company profiles

AECI
PO Box 1122
Johannesburg 2000
Phone: (011) 223-1586
Fax: (011) 223-1562

Summary
AECI's CSI structure somewhat resembles that of the Premier Group's Social Investment Councils, with regional committees of managers and worker representatives who help to make grant decisions for projects in their areas and then monitor their grantees. The fact that AECI's CSI 'Quality of Life' budget is currently managed by a former industrial relations manager has added an extra dimension to its programmes. For in addition to grantmaking, AECI occasionally uses its in-house IR expertise to run workshops for some of the NGOs it supports to help them operate more efficiently; in one case, the company "loaned" IR experts to a large NGO to help resolve its difficulties with high staff turnover. AECI's new plans include increased emphasis on community-based environmental initiatives along with support for environmental research.

* * *

In 1993, after some 25 years with AECI, mostly in the human resources and industrial relations fields, Zandile Jakavula took over the management of the company's Quality of Life budget. This move was significant for a number of reasons. For one thing, Jakavula had worked in a number of AECI's companies at different sites nationwide, so he was already well versed in the firm's internal operations and knew about problems in most communities where employees live. For another, he has taken the rather novel approach of linking IR concerns with his administration of CSI. At a time

when many NGOs are worried whether they will have the funds to continue to operate, AECI's strategy equips them with skills to operate more effectively and anticipate future needs.

Like most large companies, AECI, which has 22 000 employees, had a general donations budget for many years. But in 1981, it decided to take a more focused, hands-on approach. It formed what it calls a "Quality of Life" (QoL) budget whose agenda was to plough 1 percent of pre-tax profits back into the communities in which the company operates, and hired a full-time manager to run it. This formula has resulted in annual CSI spending by AECI as high as R9 million in a particularly good year, but it has never dropped below R4 million. A further annual allocation of about R2 million goes into a Tertiary Education Institution (TEI) budget, which Jakavula manages, and the company also gave R1 million to the Urban Foundation for each of the past six years (1988-1994). This grant was spent in three ways: 50 percent goes into education pro- grammes, 30 percent toward infrastructure and the remainder for general support. Separately, AECI committed R25 million to the Joint Education Trust (JET), or R5 million over the five-year period of the JET's designated operation period.

The QoL budget emanates from AECI's Human Resources department and is overseen by three subcommittees: Education, Community Development and TEI. Committee members include Jakavula as well as AECI's group managers from finance, human resources, industrial relations, research and development, engineer- ing, information services, communications and safety, health and the environment. They help set policy and make major grant decisions. A fourth committee on environmental issues is to be put into place in 1995. It will support university-level research projects, general environmental education in schools and community groups and con- servation projects in communities and at game reserves. (A commu- nity participation clean-up at Alexandra township's Jukskei River is one example.) Twice a year, a funding committee of all subcommit- tee members meets to assess new policies and make major grant decisions.

Jakavula runs the day-to-day QoL budget operations with the assistance of just one full-time secretary. To make the best use of a tiny staff, he has created a new structure of seven regional commit- tees that at this writing had been in place for less than a year — too soon to evaluate its effectiveness. Each committee has six to eight members, equally divided between management and employees, who are usually shop stewards. The committees screen proposals

and recommend to Jakavula those they deem worthy of support. (The company's Free State operation does not have a committee, so Jakavula oversees its QoL allocation.)

Jakavula rarely turns them down: 'We want to strengthen and empower these committees to feel that they "own" certain projects,' he explains, although he may make modifications to the conditions of the grant. Obviously, though, recommended projects will only be approved if they fall within QoL budget criteria, and grants won't be renewed if projects do not meet expectations. Jakavula himself is responsible for evaluating national and rural projects that cannot be placed within local committees. Most grants range from R10 000 to R60 000, although the company singles out several high-impact projects each year with grants ranging upwards of R80 000.

Priorities

The education budget is divided into five funding areas: 1) science, maths and technology; 2) teacher skills upgrading; 3) facilities improvement, such as schools, libraries and laboratories; 4) English-language instruction, and 5) bursaries for Standard six and higher. Under this budget, AECI generally gives an annual grant to GCP, a programme that identifies gifted children from disadvantaged backgrounds to attend private schools. The community development budget covers four areas: 1) early childhood educare, with an emphasis on the training of educare teachers and infrastructure; 2) job creation; 3) leadership development, and 4) community facilities, such as clinics and recreation centres.

AECI's annual grant to the Growth of Children's Potential Trust (GCP), an enrichment programme for talented students from Soweto and Alexandra townships, is one of its largest: around R280 000 per annum. READ (see READ's Profile, from p176) gets even more: in 1993 it received R395 000, with special support for a programme of conferences and workshops for teachers and project coordinators. The company is an exclusive funder of a laboratory at the Peninsula Technikon, with an R800 000 grant ranging over five years; scheduled for completion in November 1994, it will be named after AECI. A school upgrading project in Tembisa township, which supplies many employees to AECI, cost R92 000. In this instance, the company used its own technicians to do the job. And, finally, the company funds the Matric Re-Write School in Durban, for a current annual grant of R160 000.

Impact of RDP

A key effect of the RDP on CSI policy at AECI, as Jakavula sees it, is the need to publicise the QoL budget, not just with anecdotal information but full disclosure on spending. Although past annual reports contained no information on the company's CSI, Jakavula has recommended a change in this approach: 'With the RDP, companies are expected to be seen to be helping, and if employees are also to be aware of this, we should publicise it in internal journals and the press.' While *Prospect*, AECI's in-house magazine, has discussed QoL projects and made the QoL budget the subject of a special issue in Winter 1991, Jakavula is proposing that future editions of the magazine include a complete breakdown of funded projects and the amount spent on them.

Monitoring: Setting the terms in advance

To assure project accountability, AECI specifies in its grants letter how funds are to be used and visits project sites in advance of making decisions. Local committee members make follow-up visits three or four times a year (the company gives some paid time off for committee work), and Jakavula tries to visit every project at least once a year. It's obviously in the company's interest to help a floundering project it funded work better. So, for instance, when Jakavula became aware that a small business development project in Tembisa to which the company had given support was not working well, he arranged with the Small Business Unit of the University of the Orange Free State to set up a curriculum in basic management skills and create a regular system of report-backs and statistics on how the programme was progressing.

In another instance, AECI learned that a specific programme of READ that it was funding had an unreasonably high staff turnover. 'We felt that the programme couldn't work if there were too many new faces all the time,' Jakavula says. So he met with READ's Executive Director Cynthia Hugo to analyse the problem and found that it was quite basic: salaries were too low. The company increased funding for salaries and put READ's staff into a special training programme in conflict resolution managed by AECI's industrial relations department.

A partnership process

As a veteran of AECI, Jakavula knows the company intimately and also knows what it takes to run an effective CSI programme. For one thing, he says, the person needs to be involved in community development and be committed to positive change; and for another, he or she should fit in to the communities and understand their dynamics — especially the fact that change does not occur overnight. 'Things take time, and you'll soon lose interest if you're not patient,' Jakavula says. But projects move faster if *people* are developed in the process, he feels, and that is why AECI's QoL programme is so hands-on.

Furthermore, Jakavula sees CSI as a partnership rather than a one-way giving process in which a company makes people 'bend down on their knees and ask for money. People have ideas and vision but they need the resources that we have. They need to be able to see themselves as equal partners with us, and not us as the boss.' By the same token, the company must be consistent and come through on any promises it makes, whether for a grant or a visit, and not promote false hopes. 'You cannot rely on the telephone, you need to meet face-to-face,' insists Jakavula. 'People need to be recognised by those of us from big business.'

As for the question of whether a black person is better equipped than a white person to run CSI, Jakavula has a quick reply. 'Most managers haven't been to townships and don't understand what's lacking there,' he says. 'If everything else works properly, a black CSI manager can contribute more since he or she often speaks from the heart.' Yet he shares the same stresses of his counterparts of every race: the need to turn down the growing number of appeals coming his way, many of which are for very credible projects.

Jakavula loves his job: 'You make friends, you're part of a development and you feel good when a project yields results because you've been part of it,' he says. And 'you get to travel a lot and that develops you as a human being. I have friends everywhere in the country.'

Jakavula is an avid networker. AECI is part of a coalition of six companies with East Rand operations that contributed to the construction of the Tembisa Business Centre, a skills training and job creation programme (mentioned above). This project, to which AECI contributed R150 000, one-sixth of the cost, has helped unemployed people in a politically divided area to start their own small businesses, and has promoted stability. The company also donated R75 000 over a three-year period for business management courses. In another instance, AECI joined Coca-Cola South Africa in funding a new library building and librarian-training programme in Lebowa. In August 1994 Jakavula was elected to the first board of SAGA.

Jakavula is one of the trustees in a joint project with four other corporate partners with operations in or around Newcastle in Natal. The project involved the construction of a training centre for teacher upgrading, skills training, career guidance and science and maths programmes. AECI contributed more than R200 000.

Future visions

Jakavula expects that AECI will be pressurised by more groups for support. He believes that capacity-building for NGOs rather than more funding is one of the directions AECI's CSI programme will follow. 'Even if they don't see a need for this now, they *will* later on,' he says. This will be especially so if NGOs are forced to retrench staff or reorganise in the "shake-out" process now under way — and as government makes new policies to meet the demands of the RDP. In addition, some unions are now trying to organise NGO employees, and Jakavula believes he can make a contribution in helping provide NGOs with IR expertise to become more effective as managers.

Anglo American and De Beers' Chairman's Fund
PO Box 61587
Marshalltown 2107
Phone: (011) 638-9111
Fax: (011) 638-2455

Summary

The Anglo American and De Beers Chairman's Fund is South Africa's largest corporate philanthropy, not surprising since the group of companies that fund it represent the nation's largest business consortium. There are no priority areas; the fund's most recent social investment report says, simply, that the "terms of reference are of the most general kind: to support any cause or project which is considered to be socially constructive". Unlike the other CSI programmes profiled here, the Fund focuses on making donations only. One of its principal strengths, apart from the capacity to make very large gifts, is its ability to make decisions quickly so that projects may proceed.

*   *   *

Money talks when the Anglo American and De Beers Chairman's Fund delivers cheques, which can be in the millions of rand, and the fund is South Africa's largest corporate philanthropist. Executive director Michael O'Dowd, a corporate director of Anglo American who has headed the fund since it was created in 1973, seems to revel in being a contrarian. Shunning the tendency of some CSI programmes, like those at Gencor, Liberty Life and Nedcor, to engage staff directly in projects, the fund is involved almost exclusively in making donations and, says O'Dowd, leaves all programme operations to recipients.

'We want communities to own and control the projects,' he says. In addition, Anglo 'sees no point to defining CSI', preferring to restrict itself to grantmaking while keeping guidelines as broad and flexible as possible. (These guidelines bar grants linked to business promotion, staff training or projects that are limited to employees and their dependants.)

From being mainly a welfare-support fund until 1973, the Chairman's Fund now sees itself as a proactive body, in some cases helping to form organisations through major grants. It was *the* initial donor to the READ Educational Trust, now one of South Africa's largest literacy NGOs. Anglo American Corporation (*not* the Fund) was a major backer of both the Urban Foundation and JET. Anglo and its affiliated companies pledged R50 million per year for five years to JET, equal to 1,5 percent of dividends (see the Joint Education Trust Profile on p167).

The Chairman's Fund is divided into two types: a "responsive" fund which reacts to an appeal and cannot create anything new, and a "Special Projects Fund" which joins three elements: a grant, a "constituency" which will benefit from it, and an organisation with the expertise to fulfil the grant's goals. Such projects include clinics or schools, for which the Fund covers capital costs and is often the only financial sponsor, although other donors sometimes become partners. There is also a Chairman's Fund Educational Trust which donates solely to secondary and tertiary education and comes from a separate budget. It mainly supports black colleges, particularly in rural areas.

Giving priorities are not set in concrete; although most grants go to education, followed by health and social investment, these may change as the government embarks on new programmes. 'We've been spending money in areas which we thought were neglected by government; in another year's time, things could be very different,' comments O'Dowd.

For the most part, organisations approach the Fund for grants with a full proposal. If they don't have the capacity to write one but their programme seems worthwhile, staff members will help them prepare it. Once a grant is given, 'We don't do a great deal of monitoring. That's very expensive,' O'Dowd says. 'But the grapevine is very effective and if anything is going wrong we hear about it. There have been cases where we intervened elaborately and became deeply involved. But this isn't part of our function.'

Keeping projects independent

One reason O'Dowd objects to such involvement is that he feels projects then become more the property of the donor than the organisation that runs them. He has a similar feeling about community trusts: 'We don't support them and we disapprove of them,' says O'Dowd. 'If you ask "real" community leaders to serve on a trust, their constituency expects results and the trust could become corrupted or paralysed. Some trusts have gotten bad reputations for being too slow. And the question of constituencies is a problem. We have contact with a very wide range of community leaders. Some are real, some aren't.'

Apart from its size, the Chairman's Fund considers itself unique in two other ways: its fast reaction time and its very broad guide-lines, which mean that 'We never have to tell anyone they don't meet them,' says O'Dowd. For a request of up to R25 000 the Fund can normally respond within two weeks, as long as the applicant can answer questions promptly and accurately. A well-motivated and urgent appeal seeking between R30 000 and R80 000 can get an answer in one or two months. A much larger request can get a fast response if it is for an urgent project, but generally requires much more time because the Fund wants a role in structuring how the grant is allotted and used.

How it works

The Fund has a full-time staff of 13, of whom 5 have executive responsibility to receive, evaluate and monitor appeals and propose grants to a committee of senior executives. O'Dowd says that 'We do *not* practise affirmative action at the Fund — we're merit-based only,' and at the time of the interview the staff had no black members. Since then, an Indian man was hired to replace a white Fund executive who had left. Women have done fairly well here; two of the five Fund executives are female. O'Dowd feels there can be some problems if a black person is named to head a CSI department; the person could be 'much more vulnerable to a wide range of pressures and can be put into a dangerous position. The greatest problem could relate to traditional, cultural and family reasons not to say no to an appeal.'

When the Fund seeks new employees, it excludes candidates who seem 'too highly motivated, i.e. bleeding hearts, because if you care too much, it could destroy you because you feel you can't do enough. You have to turn people down,' says O'Dowd. 'You have to be systematic, regular and efficient. You also have to look out for a person who wants access to power, to be Father Christmas. So we look for thoroughly balanced people with outgoing personalities and basic competencies.'

Anglo American's only employee involvement comes from the controlling committee of about 12 senior executives who attend six meetings a year to discuss major grants and update projects. The committee's only black member at this writing was Anglo director Don Ncube. Otherwise there is no employee (including trade union) input.

Almost-full disclosure

Anglo American allocates one page in its annual report to Community Investment, which includes full reporting on its grant giving, and on occasion has published a separate grant report. (Separate space is devoted to the firm's extensive small business subcontracting programme, which is regarded as one of South Africa's most effective.) This report gives an anecdotal overview of the year's major giving projects and then provides a detailed breakdown of grant expenditures.

Funds available are based on dividends. For 1993, the Chairman's Fund and Educational Trust approved 900 grants worth R39,4 million (up from R36,8 million in 1992, but down from R58,7 million in 1991, when the group had higher earnings). Giving broke down as follows: 33 percent to tertiary education; 26 percent to secondary education; 1,4 percent for primary education; 5,9 percent towards research; 3,7 percent to general charities; 13,6 percent to cultural, social and "miscellaneous" groups; 8 percent towards community development and health; and 8,4 percent for non-formal education and training.

Despite the Fund's preference, at times it has had to take a hands-on role in sponsored projects. When internal divisions in the administering council at Grace College, a community-sponsored private school in Protea, Soweto, threatened to paralyse its operations, the Fund arranged for Don Ncube to sit on Grace's council and help straighten out its problems. The Fund, which covered the construction of a new building, dislikes becoming so involved because of the 'danger of a dependency syndrome', according to O'Dowd. 'We don't want to give the impression that organisations can keep asking for more.'

The job gets easier

Such intervention is rarely needed, and O'Dowd finds that his job has become easier over time. For one thing, there are many more good groups to fund, which helps explain why, like so many of his counterparts, he says that 'I love my job. In the early years it was difficult to find good projects and now it's easier to be a donor. First, there's the obvious point that you're making a difference where the need is great. Second, it gives you a view of society much wider than most people get and shows on the whole how much constructive work is going on. And there's so much opportunity to meet grass-roots people.

'The change over all these years is spectacular,' he continues. 'The essential change consists of and stems from the enormous rise of community initiatives. In the early 1970s we were dealing mainly with old-fashioned established welfare organisations. If there was to be grassroots work, the initiative came from outside the communities and a big problem was to get bona fides from within them.' This situation began to change in the late 1970s and has accelerated in numbers, depth and quality, particularly, notes O'Dowd, in rural areas. These developments have prompted the Fund to reduce support for traditional recipients in favour of more grassroots types of organisations.

One such group is Build a Better Society (BABS), based in the Western Cape. The Fund provided 50 percent of start-up funds to BABS when it was a one-man operation. Now a national organisation that mobilises poor communities to undertake self-help projects, it also trains other groups with similar goals. The community of Kewtown, where BABS started, had the highest crime rate in Cape Flats but now has one of the lowest.

Apart from possibly changing its priorities as the new government clarifies its own, the Anglo American and De Beers Chairman's Fund anticipates different types of interaction with NGOs (and possibly fewer to work with, if the government takes over some of their functions) and legislative reform that will simplify the donations process. The current Fund-Raising Act 'is grossly oppressive', finds O'Dowd. 'The old guys didn't want competitors, and the limited tax deductibility biases donations towards certain areas and harms other, including health and social welfare.' He believes the Act should be repealed in part because 'it lulls the public into a false sense of security that a certain organisation has been investigated and is being monitored, and that's not true'. It also keeps legitimate organisations from legally raising funds.

Supporting informal networks

Anglo American has refused to join the grantmakers' association SAGA. At its launch, O'Dowd objected to what he called 'taxation without representation', since member companies would have had an equal vote on policy decisions even though membership fees were to be set on a sliding scale based on the size of their donations budget. (The fee structure has since changed.) O'Dowd also feels that South Africa did not need a new bureaucracy when informal CSI networks already do what he says SAGA wants to formalise.

BMW South Africa
PO Box 2955
Pretoria 0001
Phone: (012) 529-2272
Fax: (012) 529-2575

Summary
BMW's principal CSI focus is employee-centred. Its distinctive accomplishment is the creation of an Employee Child Care Centre which serves nearly 100 employees' children. The idea for the Centre was generated by employees, who also raise money through a bi-monthly raffle to cover most of its operating costs. Although BMW pays the Centre's staff salaries, employees shoulder the responsibility for its overall maintenance, and have been consistently successful in this respect.

*   *   *

For the most part BMW limits its CSI to the communities where its 2 700 employees live, principally near its plant in Rosslyn, just outside Pretoria (mainly Garankuwa and Mabopane), and in Midrand, where corporate headquarters are located. The programme is administered by Public Affairs Manager Seth Phalatse, who has been with BMW since 1980. He and an assistant, Bongi Radebe, in a department with eight full-time staff members, each spend slightly more than half of their time on CSI. Phalatse was a member of the working group that developed the framework for SAGA.

CSI at BMW began as a management initiative in 1981, and from the outset focused on employee welfare issues, particularly housing. 'Management felt employees should appreciate the quality where they live. If they're building a R100 000 car, they shouldn't live in a shack,' Phalatse explains.

BMW divides its CSI into three categories: 1) education, 2) local community development and 3) small business. In addition, the firm loans 25 cars on a long-term basis to educational and business institutions and selected NGOs. They use them for 11 000 kilometres and the company services, maintains and insures them. Recipients include the Urban Foundation's executive director for fundraising, Nafcoc and the German Chamber of Commerce. These are 5-series cars worth about R185 000.

BMW's other support still has a connection to employee needs, even though they may be indirect. These include sponsorship of

teacher upgrading at Vista University's Centre for Cognitive Development in Verwoerdburg, which has trained more than 1 000 teachers, and PROTEC, which offers training in technical careers, with a focus on supplementary maths and science, for students in Standards eight and ten.

Centrepiece of BMW's CSI: Early Learning Centre

In 1983, BMW's union proposed that management support the formation of an early childcare facility for employees' children. After negotiating this issue, both parties agreed to set up an early learning centre. Company management would build it at plant premises and pay staff salaries (one principal and four teachers) as long as employees took the responsibility for equipment, food and upkeep. To do so, employees launched a raffle and raised the start-up funds. Since then, employees have sponsored a bi-monthly raffle, selling tickets for R20 each — and have never had a problem meeting costs. (Ticket purchases are deducted from employees' pay cheques.)

About 100 employees' children from the ages of three until school-going age attend the Centre. More than 90 percent are black — a figure which represents the racial make-up of BMW's workforce — while white employees often have access to good childcare facilities close to home. (Phalatse adds that some white parents were reluctant to take advantage of the Centre, and just a handful of white children are enrolled.) A parents' committee sets the fee structure. Until South Africa's schools were open to children of all races, almost all of the centre's "graduates" were admitted to private schools, and in some cases BMW provided bursaries for them.

Phalatse notes that BMW South Africa operates fairly closely to the model of its German parent, IG Metal. When an investigative commission from one of the German trade unions visited the firm to see how German companies in SA conformed with their values, BMW scored positively on 11 out of 14 points, mainly related to conditions of employment. 'We were never under pressure to change our policies by the German anti-apartheid movement,' Phalatse adds.

On a cash basis BMW gives out about R1 million for community development projects and social welfare, plus in-kind gifts valued between R20 000 and R50 000, generally to assist organisations operating near BMW. Examples include an outreach initiative by Medunsa to deliver health care to rural areas; the local cripple care association; the Winterveldt Community Centre, which provides meeting rooms for local groups and teaches basic courses in sewing, knitting and related skills; and sponsorship of a house at SOS Village in Mamelodi, a children's residence which has about 12 houses for 10 children each, with a housemother and full facilities to give them a caring, stable environment. Phalatse points out that BMW was the first company to invest in a primary school in Ivory Park, an informal Midrand settlement.

In addition, BMW supports projects that extend the use of the Early Learning Centre, such as a YMCA-sponsored early learning project in which BMW invited teachers to spend two to three weeks at the Rosslyn centre.

Small business support

BMW is becoming increasingly active in small business development, supporting various training initiatives and subcontracting. It gives funding to the Small Business Centre at the University of Potchefstroom for training at offices in Johannesburg and Rosslyn (based at BMW), where courses are offered in bookkeeping, management and marketing to members of Fabcos and Nafcoc.

However, the company's subcontracting initiatives have had mixed results. This could be in part because BMW defines subcontracting as a social investment and "economic empowerment" initiative rather than part of a more concrete business strategy and has not structured it to follow strict business guidelines. In conjunction with chemical firm Hoechst South Africa, which has a small business development unit, BMW is supporting a black businessman who operates a specialty chemical firm to produce car care products and windscreen cleaners; Hoechst helps to maintain quality standards and the two firms assist in distribution.

Phalatse took a hands-on role to help the manufacturer get his operation off the ground by providing guidance on quality control and assisting him to organise business procedures. For instance, when the man had difficulty raising start-up capital BMW gave assurances that the company would provide contracts. Phalatse also visited the manufacturer's factory in Industria near Johannesburg. He saw that the man was using poor-quality labels but had made no effort to obtain better ones because his customers, mostly other small businesses, had not expressed concern. 'But *we* made a fuss,' Phalatse recalls, 'and told him to find a more reliable label supplier.' In addition, many of the man's suppliers were demanding advance payment for materials, a procedure which Phalatse believed was based on the fact that the man was black, and he helped sort this problem out. Ultimately, 'we resolved the "teething" difficulties and he's doing well,' Phalatse says.

On a less labour-intensive basis, BMW aids small businesses by subcontracting car-washing in its Rosslyn plant to a white woman, thereby creating jobs for 10 women. And at the time of our interview, the company was about to subcontract the washing of its Midrand premises and cars to a black woman, with the ultimate goal of sub-contracting the cleaning of its entire company premises to her. In addition, the firm has subcontracted the cleaning of laundry uniforms to a black woman in Rosslyn and eventually plans to subcontract glove-mending. To find some of these operators, BMW links up with Nafcoc and various local chambers of commerce and with Fabcos.

Day-to-day management

Like most CSI departments, BMW's is deluged with requests. Phalatse and Bongi Radebe review all of them and then she makes a closer evaluation of those that they may want to follow through on. 'We also work closely with union guys on proposals and invite their input,' says Phalatse.

Monitoring projects consists of taking active involvement in them, serving on committees or boards of the organisations BMW supports. For instance, Phalatse sits on the working committee of the Centre for Cognitive Development, Radebe sits on its training com-mittee, and once a year the company arranges a feedback session from teachers and inspectors on programme progress, so far with positive results.

How he got there

Seth Phalatse is a natural communicator, so although his working career did not begin in public affairs it is not surprising that it is where he has ended up. After leaving school in 1965 he became a clerk at Continental China, and then in 1973 joined the company Metal Box, where he started as a clerk and eventually became a per-sonnel and recruitment officer. BMW headhunted Phalatse in 1980 for its personnel department, but he later moved into industrial rela-tions and welfare, earning a labour relations diploma from Unisa at the same time. He joined BMW just when labour relations was becoming a "hot" area in South Africa. When BMW went on strike in 1984, the firm identified poor communications as one cause of the strike, and Phalatse applied for, and got, an appointment as a com-pany communications officer — the first black person at BMW to hold this post.

One of his innovations was to create an in-house "video newsletter" for employees which he wrote and produced. 'We thought this was the best way to get through to employees and alternate it with a written newsletter,' he says. Each month the videos were shown in the townships to employees and their families; in Garankuwa this also included live entertainment. Around 1986, when BMW decided to formalise its CSI programme (which was previously run by a social worker who reported to the company's human resources department), Phalatse took charge: by then he had been promoted to public relations manager. He has been a senior manager in public affairs since 1989, and was given more responsibilities and more staff.

In addition to CSI, Phalatse's department arranges all BMW visits and plant tours and he is also involved with lobbying, bringing together opinion-leaders and senior management, a task that requires him to be very knowledgeable on socio-political developments.

Being black makes an obvious difference in Phalatse's effectiveness, he feels, both in general public relations and in administering CSI. 'Black people understand problems of the communities we're trying to help and are better judges of what must be done,' he maintains. Still, 'You must be very disciplined and consistent and unbiased, and you must also be open-minded and able to talk to people.'

Like many of his colleagues, Phalatse sometimes finds his responsibilities overwhelming. 'We can always do more than what we're doing. Government should be able to do some projects that we do. The new government will have mammoth tasks; if I was solely doing CSI, I'd be worried. Government should ensure equal and quality education. If we stop any projects and focus on employee welfare, our work would improve, and companies could focus on internal needs.'

At this writing BMW was reviewing a proposal to revamp its CSI to be in line with the RDP. An RDP Council consisting of senior management from Finance, Procuring, Human Resources and Marketing, plus its trade union, was been established to "own" the BMW RDP.

BP Southern Africa
BP Centre
Thibault Square
Cape Town
Phone: (021) 408-2434
Fax: (021) 214-635

Summary

A wholly-owned subsidiary of chemical giant British Petroleum, BP Southern Africa (BPSA) has taken a people-centred approach to CSI which extends to its employees, a concept inspired by National Public Affairs Manager, Mary-Jane Morifi. Unlike many CSI managers who followed a path up the corporate ladder, Morifi moved into CSI after creating and running an NGO and doing other community-based work. Under her direction BPSA has encouraged employee community involvement by creating a database of employee skills that enables the company to match them with needy organisations. And in addition to producing a comprehensive Business Report which describes its CSI programmes, BPSA's public affairs unit publishes an easy-to-read guide which describes how the company spends its CSI money and encourages employees how to get more information or suggest projects for possible funding.

* * *

Around 1991, while directing the Durban-based Ecumenical Bursary Fund, Mary-Jane Morifi was having a conversation with a friend from the corporate world. It was a particularly bloody time in Natal and Morifi had just set up a special Crisis Bursary Fund to help families who had lost everything in the violence. 'He was with BP, we were talking about work, and I asked him, what are *you* doing about what's going on,' she says. She had already established an NGO called Planned Route Into Science and Maths (PRISM), which provides tutorial assistance to matric students, and had found that while overseas embassies and groups readily provided funds, local companies were not pulling their weight.

'He gave me a very unsatisfactory answer,' says Morifi. 'I didn't see BP having any impact.' So she gave him her CV, and, soon after, was invited to BP's Durban office, where she was offered a public relations job. She was not able to accept the job as she was expecting a baby at the time, and Morifi instead joined the

Mangosuthu Technikon as senior public affairs director of its foundation.

Still, Morifi felt unhappy with local corporate CSI programmes and believed she could do a better job if given the chance. 'I felt some companies were irresponsible in the way they gave money,' she comments. 'I saw organisations that weren't very good getting big grants because of who they knew and other good groups that couldn't get funded.'

The next time BP contacted her, it was with an offer she couldn't refuse: to head the company's public affairs division at its Cape Town headquarters. The job included running BPSA's CSI, which also covers Lesotho and Swaziland. Morifi had always wanted to return to Cape Town, where she had studied, and she joined the company in October 1993. Her responsibilities also include general public affairs for BP Southern Africa and the company's affirmative action programme.

Nowadays, Morifi heads a staff of 14, some in the Cape Town head office and others in Johannesburg (which takes in Gauteng and the Free State) and Durban. All CSI projects are consciously designed to have a "win-win" result for both company and recipients. 'There has to be something in it for us,' she points out. 'It's a selfish way of doing things, but you need to assure that the environment is conducive to doing business.'

Even so, the company has used its clout to influence social change not directly related to its business — although the public relations dividend is high. More than 20 years ago — long before Morifi was on the scene — BPSA's sponsorship of the Soccer Top 8 tournament was conditioned on the racial integration of soccer, and it succeeded. The company successfully challenged the Group Areas Act when it built the Springfield Terrace housing complex in District Six. Some of the original residents of the area, forced out under the apartheid regime, were able to move back.

Original approaches: Volunteerism and CSI bonuses
Under Morifi, the company has taken further strides. After just more than a year at BPSA when she was interviewed for this book, she had introduced several new approaches to CSI not practised at other South African companies.

One is to promote employee volunteer involvement in local communities, a form of corporate sponsorship rare in South African companies. In some cases, this means that BP will make a grant to an organisation in which an employee actively donates time.

'Instead of imposing our projects on communities, we want to find out and help projects that our employees are involved in,' she says.

In February 1994, a few months after she went on staff, Morifi worked with the company's Market Research department on an employee survey to assess their current or potential involvement to do community work. The survey sought information on which employees were involved in community projects, what these projects were, what types of work employee-volunteers were doing, what skills they had to offer, and whether employees who were *not* doing volunteer work would be interested in starting if the company could identify a good project for them. (This is a model practised at some US companies, some of which run volunteer referral centres to match employees with local community groups.)

'When you volunteer with organisations you get to learn new skills not taught in the workplace. And managers get information that an employee is involved in community work,' she says. It helps promote a greater public awareness "ethos" generally absent in South African companies.

The survey resulted in substantial information for the company. First, it provided a database of community-based organisations that Morifi's team might not otherwise have known about. Second, it assessed project needs and the skills BP's staff can provide. For instance, if an organisation needs bookkeeping assistance, the database can identify a staff bookkeeper who might be willing to volunteer with that group. 'So instead of spending money, you get a useful way to use people,' she says. Furthermore, the spouses of some employees included returned exiles without work permits but who have excellent skills that can add value to community groups.

In addition, the company "rewards" itself, through its CSI budget, when employees perform well. Under this plan, BPSA not only offers performance bonuses (almost equivalent to a 14th cheque) to employees who meet or surpass targets, but *matches* these bonuses in the form of a donation to the CSI budget. Introduced in 1994 as part of campaign to improve performance, the system resulted in an extra R4 million added to the CSI coffer — a doubling of its budget for that year! It was a good year for BPSA, says Morifi, who believes it is the only company to make this type of CSI match.

And, finally, BP publishes a brochure on its community investments, *How Your Company Spends its Money in the Community,* which is easy to read, explains social spending categories, describes a number of funded projects and tells employees how to contact the company's regional affairs managers if they know of projects they think merit funding support. The brochure predates Morifi's arrival at BPSA.

How BPSA's CSI works

BPSA allocates the lion's share of CSI spending — 43 percent — to education, with the rest divided between sport projects (16 percent), environmental issues (11 percent), community development projects (10 percent), job creation (7 percent) and the balance in a general fund that includes culture and youth projects.

The number of major projects funded is relatively small: just 35 at a given time, says Morifi. But these are projects her staff services with personal assistance as well as money. Donations from R500 to R5 000 to several dozen general welfare organisations do not require hands-on involvement. Three regional managers have substantial autonomy over CSI for grants up to R20 000 while Morifi makes decisions on national projects.

In line with a focus on mass education in health and safety, BPSA donated R1 million of the R6 million cost of the multimedia "Soul City" health project, which includes a television series that ran in mid-1994, radio programmes and extensive print materials. This grant made the company the principal corporate sponsor. With major backing from Unicef and the Open Society Foundation, "Soul City" dramatised key health concerns such as AIDS, pre- and post-natal care, paraffin poisoning and other health issues of special concern to poorer communities. The company will be a major sponsor of a series sequel which will be broadcast in 1996. (An interesting aspect of its funding is Nestlé's agreement to fund the printing of project-related pamphlets on breast-feeding. Morifi calls this Nestlé's response to an international boycott protesting the company's promotion of baby formula in developing countries where mothers were less likely to afford it and should be encouraged to breast-feed.)

BPSA's next largest grant was for a paraffin safety campaign, launched in October 1994. This aimed to prevent paraffin poisoning among children in poorer communities, who sometimes drink paraffin from bottles that they think contain cold drink. Paraffin is one of BP's most popular products, but it is often sold in beverage bottles and, says Morifi, 16 000 cases of paraffin poisoning (and some deaths) among children are reported each year; she believes that many more cases are not reported. Most victims are from informal settlements where medical care is limited. The company allocated just under R800 000 to fund the production of four million plastic safety caps (in BP green) that can fit on the types of bottles in which paraffin is often sold, along with bright plastic gummed labels to put on these bottles to indicate clearly that they contain paraffin and not a beverage.

In addition, the company funded a massive media and education campaign to publicise the programme. It includes visits to hundreds of schools clinics and ladies' clubs to educate children, health workers and community leaders on the project. The company challenged other oil, chemical, pharmaceutical and detergent manufacturers to take part, but none had signed on at the time it was launched.

Understanding NGO dynamics

Morifi's NGO experience gives her special insights in the internal workings of the organisations BPSA assists and has helped limit the types of failures that some corporate donors have experienced. When a big grant is made, the money is allocated in instalments, regular reports must be submitted and someone in her department gets involved, usually by sitting on the organisation's board and making frequent project visits.

This system isn't foolproof, however; at one point BPSA planned to support a substantial community education computer project, especially after receiving glowing reports on its progress — written, it turned out, by someone who had not visited its premises. An evaluator who *did* visit was appalled by what he saw and recommended that funding be pulled — and that the organisation (which Morifi would not name) be liquidated. 'They never paid taxes, were in great debt, had no accounting system and people didn't come to work,' she says. By then, fortunately, BPSA had only committed a small amount.

Job-related CSI: Part of a trend

In a trend among companies to link their business needs with CSI, BP is supporting a new "Township MBA" programme which trains entrepreneurs in preparing business plans. Most of them are involved in retail or resale businesses, and the company particularly seeks to support vendors of BP products, such as paraffin and gas. Some of these have become very successful and sell the products through BP Community Energy Centres. Pilot projects are currently running in Johannesburg and Port Elizabeth.

These linkages bring value to the company as well as communities. The company is also linking its bursary programme to recruitment needs, so will place more emphasis on training potential engineers, chemists and other professionals that it needs.

'I try to be realistic in my projects,' Morifi comments. 'I always think of the company *and* the community; a programme has to work for both.' Moreover, with a limited budget, she has to make sure projects produce dividends for many parties. To this end, Morifi herself will often advise projects on how to work more efficiently. Sometimes she'll give them her time in lieu of money.

While Morifi acknowledges that she has some advantages in being black, she believes she is especially effective because she has 'had exposure and done a "tour of duty" in communities'. Her networks are diverse and she knows which organisations can deliver. And as BPSA, like other companies, refines its approach to the RDP, Morifi is well positioned to identify those organisations that are doing good RDP-related work and should be supported.

Coca-Cola South Africa
PO Box 9999
Johannesburg 2000
Phone: (011) 488-0619
Fax: (011) 488-0711

Summary
Coca-Cola South Africa's CSI is distinguished by the innovative "multiplier" style developed by social responsibility programmes manager Eunice Sibiya. A Coca-Cola Corporate Social Responsibility Network, known as the Joint Project Participation Scheme, encourages franchised bottlers associated with the company to engage in CSI and rewards the best projects they support. Network members receive a newsletter, funding from the Coca-Cola CSI budget to help at least one major project per bottler, and are invited to an annual CSI seminar. Coca-Cola also offers training in how to run an effective CSI programme, one of few companies to do so. Sibiya's approach illustrates a practical way to make a limited CSI budget go far and proves that a company does not have to be large (some of the affiliates are small family-owned firms) to be effective in a community.

*   *   *

At this writing, the Coca-Cola Company, which had divested from South Africa in 1986, had recently announced plans to return. Under the new arrangement, Coca-Cola repurchased National Beverage Services, master franchise holder for South Africa of the products of the Coca-Cola Company. As a result of the reinvestment, Coca-Cola South Africa's CSI programme is set to expand, beginning in 1995-6. This profile examines the programme run by Eunice Sibiya, who at the time that this book was prepared headed a two-person department with a budget of R3,5 million. Her staff has since doubled. Although the firm was then known as NatBev, this profile uses its new name, Coca-Cola South Africa.

Sibiya's hallmark has been to develop an imaginative strategy to make limited funds go far. She has done this by creating the 'Coca-Cola Corporate Social Responsibility (CSR) Network' of the 33 bottlers who do business with Coca-Cola Southern Africa Division. Some participating firms are family-owned operations with few employees. But all are encouraged to become involved, through CSI seminars, newsletters and an annual awards programme. The network serves three main functions: it promotes a better relationship between the franchised bottlers and Coca-Cola (master franchise holder); fosters a social conscience among small businesses that often have neither the time nor resources on their own to engage in CSI, and, of course, promotes Coca-Cola's products in the communities that are being helped. The bottom line is never absent.

Sibiya has gained recognition for CSI as a key business function at the company. In 1994, she convinced top executives to fund a two-day CSI seminar for Coca-Cola's franchised bottlers at the Mount Grace Hotel resort. Sibiya intends to make the seminar an annual event to discuss CSI in South Africa and to honour the most creative programmes with awards.

Coca-Cola has a policy of almost full disclosure and publishes a separate social responsibility report — a holdover, perhaps, from Sullivan Code days — which describes some of the major projects it funds, lists all other recipients, and provides an overview of its budget, but no details on how much each grantee received. The report discusses the CSR Network and listed winners in its first competition in 1991. The three top winners got cash bonuses of R10 000, R5 000 and R3 000 as part of their prize. The money is for investment in each winner's domestic CSR projects.

The structure of CSI at Coca-Cola is as follows: although the actual CSI programme consists of just Sibiya and a full-time assistant (the two of them do what four people did prior to Coca-Cola's disinvestment), she has developed a network of franchised bottling companies around Southern Africa, including Namibia, Botswana, Swaziland and Lesotho. Coca-Cola sets the tone by defining CSI very broadly: investment in the future. 'For the company to survive we need to share resources — time, money and expertise — to improve quality of life, And we don't expect an immediate economic return,' says Sibiya. The budget is 1 percent of post-tax profit. This sum has grown substantially since 1986, when the first CSI budget was just R112 500. At that point its CSI went mainly toward higher education. These days, a separate Coca-Cola Tertiary Education Fund of just over R1 million, run by a company director, provides grants to universities and technikons.

Coca-Cola's CSI focuses on three areas:
1. Ongoing projects that the company will always support with donations, mainly welfare organisations involved with childcare, the aged and related areas;
2. Projects in education, community development or entrepre-

neurship that entail direct involvement, either short term (one or two years) or over a longer, phased-in period; and

3. *Ad hoc*, contingency items that were not planned in advance but are considered essential.

The 1994 budget of R3,5 million allocated nearly 47 percent for education, 28 percent for community projects and 25 percent for business development.

Not scoring points

Sibiya, who joined what became National Beverage Service in 1988 after Coca-Cola disinvested, developed a programme that was *not* designed, as the Signatory companies' often were, to score points. With fewer financial resources and the desire to spend half of her time on-site, Sibiya took a more holistic approach to CSI. Rather than look at discreet categories, she believes CSI projects must embrace interrelated concerns. 'Education isn't isolated from homes and family life — so we also invest in health and nutrition. And we build schools near homes. You can't support education without also thinking about family needs,' Sibiya maintains.

At the 1994 annual Coca-Cola CSR network conference, held shortly before the national elections, participants were treated to an analysis of post-election political and social issues and brainstormed on how CSI was likely to change under the new government. CSI managers from AECI, Eskom and Gencor described how their programmes operate. An industrial manager, who was previously a trade union official, discussed worker reactions to CSR. The 1994 winner was Peninsula Beverages (PenBev), a Western Cape bottler which was honoured for its sponsorship of three projects: Ethel's Place, a shelter for homeless children to which PenBev donated food when their supplies ran out; Ukhanyo Primary School, which the company, along with other local firms and volunteers, built to serve families in a squatter camp that had no school; and Safeline, a rehabilitation centre that caters for the abused and the abuser.

Coca-Cola's largest projects include the Coke Toy Box, a project developed by the Human Sciences Research Council based on an idea Sibiya had. The company donates about R500 000 per year (see the Toybox Project Profile on p182), supports a series of environmental projects to promote recycling (about R260 000 in 1994), a mobile clinic at the University of KwaZulu, the Small Enterprise Foundation in Tzaneen, and Wits University's Centre for Developing Business.

Apart from the Coca-Cola CSR Network, some projects are

generated from employees, who are kept abreast of the company's CSI through an in-house newsletter, *Beverage Buzz*, and are encouraged to make project suggestions. One such funded project was a computer centre in Kathlehong.

On occasion Sibiya collaborates on projects with counterparts at other companies. An example of this is a container school at Zonkisizwe squatter camp. A residents' committee had approached Coca-Cola with a proposal to create a primary school for 500 students. Safmarine donated 29 containers; Coca-Cola agreed to refurbish them and paid most of the cost to transport them to the site; JCI paid the balance. The residents' committee negotiated with the Transvaal Provincial Authority to lay the foundations, made the appropriate link-ups with education officials to run the school, and obtained school furniture from another firm. The school will be electrified by Eskom.

Monitoring projects with such a small staff is difficult. Sibiya tries to visit projects at least once a year or arrange for plant employees to do so. Many CSI projects have had mixed results, and sometimes experienced deep problems. In one case, the company and PenBev co-funded a new playground in Zwelithemba Township in Worcester, following a neighbourhood-instigated clean-up. It was vandalised within a year. 'No one really knows why it happened, and for us it was hurting,' Sibiya says. 'It was the first project we'd done there.' The company has since funded other programmes in the area, including a community-run childcare centre. 'We built up walls, painted it, had an "official opening" and invited representatives from local groups. So far it's intact.' But Sibiya declined an appeal to rebuild the playground.

A people person

Trained as a nurse, Sibiya had had ample experience in a "caring" profession before she switched to CSI. (Many black women in CSI have similar backgrounds, she says, because they had few other options.) She entered the private sector 'because I was frustrated and wanted to be able to use my talents freely. I wanted to work in an area where I could make decisions instead of being prescribed to.' So in 1984 she joined Carlton Paper, whose marketing department had advertised for nurses to do health education for product promotion in schools and clinics. She later was promoted to run the company's CSI. In 1987 she was retrenched, but by then she had landed her job at Coca-Cola.

There she brought the right combination of pragmatism, perseverance, innovation, communication skills and a rapport with people. 'It's not money that improves the quality of life but understanding situations and finding out how to make them work,' says Sibiya. 'But you have to have more than judgement; you have to appreciate the motivation of people who come to you even if they don't know the right way to ask for help. I'll sometimes teach people how to request funding so that they can get it from other companies.' (More black-run groups obtain funding with this assistance.)

Sibiya laughed when she was asked if she thought being black was important in running CSI effectively. While she agreed that it helps for language and cultural reasons, Sibiya does not feel that race should be a criterion in recruiting CSI professionals. 'It's not a question of black or white but having the right qualities for the job,' she believes. 'Some blacks doing CSI are more like messengers for their white boss. I don't know if it's the company culture or the person.' Then, naming a white woman with many years of experience in CSI, she notes that the key issue is knowing the communities and being in them. 'She's always out there,' says Sibiya.

Easier . . . and harder

While CSI is generally becoming a more systematic, and therefore smoother, process as NGOs and community-based organisations (CBOs) gain better skills at approaching donors, Sibiya saw how township violence in 1994 made her job more difficult. The water system was not working while she was *en route* to a project in Vosloorus, and local residents forced her to drive them to a place where they could get water. This incident scared Sibiya.

Still, she denies feeling burnout. 'I'm not getting any younger but I manage to generate the energy to do the work,' she says. 'There's so much that needs to be done and there's just not enough money to do it and we have limited time.' Fortunately, the culture at the company 'is such that I always get staff. The managing director makes the company realise that CSR is important and when we need help, we get it,' she confirms.

In addition, Sibiya feels heartened at what appears to be a new professionalism in the practice of CSI. 'There was a time when CSI was more of a handout type of thing. Some "clever" people would get money that would end up in their pockets and not in the communities,' she points out. 'Now there's a genuine desire to go out and develop communities from the grassroots. It's more hands-on, getting your hands dirty. I still feel it's the most neglected profession. It's not recognised, like public relations or accountants. There's a need to give training and accreditation, and recognition anytime you do anything that's exciting.' Still, some colleagues in other departments questioned the company's approval to hold the CSR Network Seminar at a luxury hotel. But if Coca-Cola could spend 'millions on product promotions or excursions at the Wild Coast, they shouldn't complain when we spend money at Mount Grace', Sibiya suggests.

And the payoff has been important, in sensitising bottlers to the need to consult with communities before undertaking CSI. 'The wrong people can kill a project,' Sibiya says. 'What's unique with us is the Coca-Cola CSR Network. It's very important to "sell" CSR to our companies.'

Sibiya was active in the formation of the SAGA and was elected its first chair in August 1994.

Colgate-Palmolive Foundation
PO Box 79515
Senderwood 2145
Phone: (011) 453-1453
Fax: (011) 453-2140

Summary:

US-owned Colgate-Palmolive Southern Africa established an autonomous foundation in 1992, as a proactive response to the array of political and social changes under way. This was done in part to preserve a high level of social spending that was roughly equivalent to the amount required of US companies by the Statement of Principles (formerly the Sullivan Code), which monitored the social responsibility of US companies in South Africa during the sanctions era. However, with the scrapping of the reporting requirement when sanctions were lifted in late 1993, the Foundation is focusing its programmes more sharply along specific themes, mainly children, youth development and multiculturalism, that also make it possible to market the Colgate name.

*   *   *

Colgate-Palmolive Southern Africa, a wholly-owned subsidiary of the US-based Colgate-Palmolive Company, came to South Africa in 1929 and is the nation's largest manufacturer of dental care products. With 938 employees at two plants, it is small compared to most of the companies profiled in this book, but large enough to have a well-developed CSI programme. Its head office is in Boksburg.

Over the years, the company resisted pressure in the US to disinvest from South Africa, and, in recent years, rejected a US shareholder resolution to adopt the South African Council of Churches' proposed Code of Conduct for Business Operating in South Africa. It had been one of the first signatories to the Statement of Principles, which among other things, required companies seeking a top rating to spend at least 12 percent of payroll on social investment and community development programmes. This 12 percent spending level remained in place even when local companies were confronting economic recession, work stoppages or stayaways that incurred major losses. Many companies, says Colgate-Palmolive South Africa's Linda Rowell, who runs the company's foundation, were struggling for basic survival. Even so, Colgate-Palmolive consistently earned top ratings.

Although some US-owned firms announced that they would reduce their level of social spending when sanctions were scrapped, Colgate-Palmolive pledged to maintain its own, confirms Rowell, who has run the company's CSI since 1988. In 1992, anticipating the change to a black-led government, the company formed a foundation to which it pledged more than R10 million. About 90 percent of the budget goes into projects as well as tertiary education bursaries for the children of employees. The rest covers overheads. Rowell is the foundation's only full-time staff member; she has a part-time secretary.

New priorities

From being a completely internal CSI programme that focused on needs of employees and the communities in which the company operates, Colgate-Palmolive's CSI now combines some internal CSI (including workforce involvement) with community investment. Its two areas of focus are children's education, especially pre-school programmes and township-based schools for mentally handicapped children, and multicultural youth development. The latter theme is part of an international programme by Colgate-Palmolive, and has prompted the company to expand the spectrum of communities in which it works. 'Most of our programmes were in black townships, and there was a perception that this big multinational company was just working for blacks,' Rowell said. Furthermore, as state schools and other institutions became nonracial, new opportunities are arising to invest in more areas.

Seven trustees provide input to help balance internal and external needs. Three come from the company: Gerry Nocker, Vice President, Southern Africa; Regional Finance Director Lionel Saunders; and Human Resources Manager Walter Skosana. Three are from outside: Ian Clark and Simon Aphane, both with the Centre for Developing Business, and Godfrey Mbatha, an East Rand businessmen active in local civic affairs. Rowell is the seventh.

Changes

During the state of emergency in the mid-1980s, Colgate-Palmolive protested in court the obnoxious behaviour of Boksburg's town council, which had fenced in the Boksburg Lake to bar blacks and tried to prevent the firm from running a multiracial nursery school for the children of employees and community residents. It still owns the school.

The company also attempted in those days to support black entrepreneurship with a loan programme called the Business Development Trust. Designed on a revolving system, it disbursed loans to a number of East Rand entrepreneurs, some of whom became quite successful. But, says Rowell, a number of them never repaid the loans. The company wrote off the debt and dropped the programme. This type of situation is no longer tolerated, though it conformed with the "don't pay rent" culture of the times — especially when the "landlord" was a large multinational corporation which, a programme evaluation found, was one reason participants gave for not repaying loans.

On-site, the company sponsors The Diamond Project, an internship programme which places university graduates into temporary positions to give them workplace experience. Colgate-Palmolive has placed a few graduates into full-time permanent positions, in information technology, marketing and administration. But the company has very low turnover, so the programme is not run every year, nor is it advertised. 'We once placed an ad and were deluged with applicants,' recalls Rowell. An employment agency handles the project instead.

Rowell oversees 81 projects at 60 organisations. Most funding helps communities near Colgate-Palmolive's offices. A major recipient is St Anthony's Adult Education Centre in Rieger Park. It offers day, evening and weekend courses to more than 5 000 adults in literacy, job skills, sewing, repeat matric courses and teacher upgrading; runs a substance abuse programme; sponsors a daycare centre for aged people and organises St Francis House, an AIDS Hospice in Boksburg which has been the target of lawsuits from residents who object to having the facility nearby. Colgate-Palmolive provides running costs and advice; another US firm has paid some of its legal fees.

Of course, Colgate-Palmolive supports many projects related to dental care. These include grants to university and technikon dental programmes nationwide which train dentists, dental hygienists and assistants, and funding for mobile clinics that offer dental treatment to poor patients. The company has supported community oral care programmes for more than 25 years, and children sometimes think the word "Colgate" means toothpaste. It serves double-duty by cultivating brand loyalty at a young age. 'I have to be candid, the company has to look at its return,' says Rowell. 'If they don't make products, they can't help the community.' Colgate-Palmolive will fund a two-chair "dental coach" on the Transnet Health Train which will be travelling around South Africa and offering clinical services in underprivileged communities from April 1995.

Intercultural interactions

Among the children's intercultural programmes Colgate-Palmolive funds are Independent Projects Trust (IPT), the Race Relations and Leadership Initiative (RALI) Group and the Colgate Care Project. IPT sponsors weekend 'Unity Through Youth' camps for students in Standards Eight and Nine. Rowell recounts how one weekend in the Magaliesburg, which brought together white students from Boksburg, coloured students from Reiger Park and black students from Vosloorus, had an unexpected dividend. 'I had phoned the Boksburg Municipal Transport office to arrange a bus, and the bus driver, who was an Afrikaner, came by and choked and swallowed when he saw who he about to take away,' she recalls. 'But he had a great time and asked to do it again, and was our driver on a weekend to the Drakensberg.'

RALI runs a year-long leadership-training and job-preparation project for high school students nationwide. These include meetings, weekend camps, team groups and an end-of-year gathering. Colgate-Palmolive sponsors its East Rand programme and Rowell attends many of its meetings.

The Colgate Care Project (Children's Advancement through Relationships and Education) takes Standard Four students on weekends away. This is a vulnerable age for children, and Rowell is fascinated by the project. In its first sequence it sponsored field trips for 10 children each from Indian, black, white and coloured schools in Boksburg. Their parents must join a parent committee and help their children in a community project, while the children must get involved in school projects. Colgate-Palmolive donated products such as cleaning materials and asked other companies to donate supplies.

In 1994, the Foundation announced Colgate's Youth for South Africa programme to honour the most innovative and constructive youth groups in the country. Modelled on the parent company's 22-year-old Youth for America campaign, the local programme emphasises self-help projects. The Foundation donates R23 000 in awards, including prizes of R2 500, R1 000 and R500, to the top three winners and many more awards of R100 and R50.

But money isn't all; Rowell serves on the board of many organisations Colgate-Palmolive supports and makes numerous site visits, in part to ensure accountability by those groups. This time-intensive aspect of her job is, she says, the only way to evaluate success or failure, which she judges not on a 'cent for cent' basis but seeing where money goes. 'Lots of people aren't good at writing reports, so we must do more than write cheques,' she says.

Employee involvement is encouraged. Some employees give time informally to the Kleinfontein Children's Home, which houses homeless children of all races. More formal is Colgate's "adopt-a-school" partnerships with seven East Rand township schools, in which employees with children at the school must get involved in order for the company to donate money. In 1992, Rowell recruited four black employees to run a workforce survey to find out which schools employees' children attended and the potential for parents to become involved; she got about 80 percent back. She then gave the parent's committee full discretion to run the adopt-a-school budget as long as it met specific criteria. The Foundation released R200 000 to buy books, equipment and sports equipment, and covered the expenses to paint classrooms and make repairs.

Getting the adopt-a-school programmes to run effectively, however, was a difficult process; although individual committee members were very involved, they often had problems getting other parents to give time. Rowell finds that employees who volunteer for such projects are self-starters who are highly motivated to advance themselves. They often come to her through the company's Employee Educational Assistance Programme and complete diplomas or acquire credentials that enable them to advance from semi-skilled jobs to skilled positions and further up the ranks. At one point Colgate-Palmolive's trade unions — mainly the Chemical Workers Industrial Union — pressurised the company for control of the CSI budget. The company would not agree, and Rowell says that she keeps the union informed and invites members to participate.

Networking is key

Rowell is an active networker, often with other US firms, such as 3M, Tupperware, Otis and John Deere. (The American Chamber of Commerce may form a social responsibility committee to encourage such networking.) Rowell also co-operates with smaller companies in the Boksburg Industrialists Association on "collective" CSI projects.

Unlike some CSI managers who have a professional background, Rowell started out as an office worker and secretary. Over time, she gained skills — and a diploma — in public relations. She ran the personnel office at another US firm before she joined Colgate-Palmolive in 1988 as an assistant to its public relations manager. When her supervisor moved on, she got the job.

Despite her experience, Rowell these days finds that her work has become somewhat harder. More organisations are appealing for funds which she cannot give: 'I can't help everyone,' she says. On the other hand, 'It's easier because of the greater capacity to do networking, and programmes are getting more successful and communities are more responsible.' At moments when she feels close to burning out, 'I visit a project and am revived.'

Eskom Community Development Programme
PO Box 1091
Johannesburg 2000
Phone: (011) 800-2346
Fax: (011) 800-2340

Summary:

In keeping with a massive overhaul at the company which began in the mid-1980s to be more responsive to its stakeholders (and, more to the point, more attuned with political changes), Eskom has revamped its CSI into a broad-based community development programme. It has also greatly expanded its CSI budget and made efforts to be more transparent about the nature and amount of its social spending. Its 'Electricity for All' strategy aims to bring cheap electricity to townships and rural schools, in order to improve the quality of education, promote electricity as a cheaper, cleaner energy alternative for small businesses — and develop a new customer base.

*   *   *

Eskom has been recognised for its exceptional affirmative action initiatives, which, since the early 1990s, have resulted in the recruitment of some of South Africa's top black talent into key executive positions. Its CSI, likewise, has evolved markedly during this period, with a new thrust on outreach projects that promote a reformed image of the utility that used to avoid black empowerment — in the most literal sense of the word!

Not surprisingly, electrification is the main component of Eskom's CSI. In an effort to get South Africa's black communities fully electrified, and therefore more capable of economic development, Eskom has increased its CSI budget substantially every year, reaching R35 million in 1994. It has links with a small business development unit in Eskom's marketing department that provides skills and job training to aspiring small business owners.

Beyond electrification, there is a general donations budget of R1 million and R2 million to cover assorted local and national welfare groups such as hospice, disaster funds and peace initiatives. Eskom's CSI budget is not, as at some other companies, a separate fund, although CSI manager Hermien Cohn says that Eskom may create a CSI Trust which could absorb foreign funding for national programmes such as school electrification.

Partnerships

Many of Eskom's CSI projects are undertaken as partnerships with other companies. For instance, in conjunction with the Department of Education and Training, Eskom has electrified a number of schools that Gencor has built. Sanlam and Eskom joined forces to develop a complex of small shops at a squatter camp in Lawaaikamp in the Western Cape, near George, using shipping containers provided by Safmarine to house them.

Eskom admits there is an obvious self-interest to its investment in township electrification: it develops a new body of paying customers. The utility installs electricity dispensers into homes and businesses that enables customers to pre-pay for electricity. The dispensers give read-outs to indicate when it is time to pay again. Eskom has a programme to subcontract dispenser installation and other township electrification projects to black contractors. Customer representatives, who often live in the service areas, inform customers about the need to pay, but their task is not easy: some users have learned to bypass the dispensers to get free electricity.

How it works

In line with its emphasis on grassroots development, Eskom's new funding areas in 1994 included adult basic education, skills development for rural women — a particular interest of Cohn's — and water provision projects, along with job creation and entrepreneurial development programmes. They represent Eskom's desires to conform to RDP guidelines.

Eskom's CSI falls under the jurisdiction of Dawn Mokhobo, Senior General Manager for Growth and Development, one of South Africa's most influential businesswomen (and winner of the 1993 "Businesswoman of the Year" award by the Executive Women's Club of South Africa). Direct management of the programme is with Cohn, a public affairs professional who ran Eskom's school bursary programme before taking over its CSI.

Cohn has four employees at Eskom headquarters: two project managers, one financial manager who tends to the CSI budget, and one secretary, plus 10 people in the business units who spend between 30 and 100 percent of their time on community development projects. Most of Cohn's CSI staff has been with her for a long time, and they are all white. In keeping with Eskom's current hiring policy, any new recruits will be black.

Indeed, Cohn herself believes that CSI works better when

blacks are in key decision-making positions, although she also feels that a good synergy results when black and white people do CSI together. 'CSI is external affirmative action, which means doing "unequal things to make sure people can be equals",' she says.

Six members of an 11-member Community Development Committee, to which Cohn makes monthly presentations for funding approvals, are black, and four are women. Its members include management representatives from Eskom's eight operating divisions: Generation, Distribution, Electrification, Finance and Services, Human Resources, Growth and Development, Technology, and Transmission.

Part of Cohn's work involves the creation in-house of what she calls a "community development culture". Employees — Eskom had 40 000 in 1994 — learn to think about community development as part of their work. An informal process, "pockets" of activities are in place in various Eskom regional offices and at some of its power stations. Secretaries at its Johannesburg offices created an in-house fundraising project to support township pre-school programmes and an old age home. They collect money in various ways through collection boxes and gathering recyclables for sale.

In addition to direct community development, Eskom claims to be equalising access to electricity by lowering the price (Cohn says Eskom is the world's second cheapest supplier); speeding up the electrification process; improving environmental management and increasing employee participation, including trade union input. Eskom's electricity council, a company/community effort to monitor policies on electrification, now includes trade union members and women, a substantial change from the old days of white male managers who made all decisions.

Eskom's management board, as shown in the 1993 annual report, was made up only of white men, but since then the company has appointed three black board members: Bongani Khumalo as Executive Director, Human Resources; Ray Debingwa, Executive Director, Electrification, and Sam Mosikili, Executive Director, Marketing.

A long history of CSI — some of it misdirected
Eskom has always had some form of CSI, but for decades it targeted whites, principally poor Afrikaners, building schools for employees' children. In 1985 the company began the first steps towards the massive change in its corporate culture for which it is now a model.

Following a board of inquiry, Eskom undertook a structural change which included its first affirmative action initiatives, bringing blacks on board and creating regular interracial contact. The utility has taken maverick strides since then in placing blacks into visible key positions. One objective is to prevent the 'revolving door' syndrome in which black executives leave their jobs after a relatively short time when better offers come their way.

Eskom's "new South African" CSI was formally launched in 1988 with a R4 million development budget, and has grown rapidly since. A separate Educational Investment Fund, formed in 1992 with a R23 million budget, covers education from pre-primary to secondary-level education. (Bursaries for tertiary education come from a separate budget). A separate fund for tertiary support and research adds R1,5 million to Eskom's development spending. In addition, the company spent more than R300 million in 1993 on training, education and development for some 2 000 employees and bursars.

These sums are published in the company's annual report, to unions, and, says Cohn, 'to anyone who asks'. 'It's a change since 1990-1, when we were concerned about how people would "perceive" how community development funds were spent,' she says, and notes that consumer reactions have generally been positive.

Cohn has also put together a summary of Eskom's Community Development Strategy, which outlines its priorities and gives a budget overview. In conjunction with BMI Issues Management, Eskom is funding a guide on fundraising for community-based organisations.

About two-thirds of the CSI budget targets capital development, mainly to electrify DET schools. (Community Development Officer Jenny Rogers, from Eskom's Johannesburg office, says that the DET used to budget for the electrification of 10 schools in Soweto each year, although there was a backlog of hundreds. Eskom is trying to take up the slack.)

Eskom's next priority after school electrification is supporting education-oriented NGOs, mainly those doing language programmes and science, maths and technology education. Eskom targets those in areas where it has major operations and many employees: the Witbank/Middelburg area of the Eastern Transvaal, Uitenhage and Port Elizabeth in the Eastern Cape, and Bloemfontein and Kimberly in the Free State and Northern Cape.

Major recipients include READ, PROTEC, Science Education Programme (SEP), Primary Science Programme (PSP) and the Natal-based Centre for the Advancement of Science and Maths

Education (CASME), which was initiated by Shell). On the pre-school level Eskom funds agencies such as Small Beginnings, which trains early childhood educare workers and sets up pre-school centres in rural areas, mainly in Gauteng; the Western Cape-based Grassroots Educare Centre; and the Border Early Learning Centre.

Eskom monitors its social investment by requiring grantees to file semi-yearly reports describing spending on specific projects. 'If we're not satisfied with these, we'll ask our business unit people to check out the situation,' says Cohn. At one point, the READ Educational Trust was unable to employ a full-time facilitator in the Natal Midlands area, for which the company had given a grant. 'They explained that our donation was too low for them and no other companies were supporting it, so we gave more so they could provide a more comprehensive service,' explains Cohn.

Considering the scale of many of Eskom's CSI investments, some have inevitably failed or stumbled. In one instance, the company had agreed to donate an empty building it owned near Grahamstown to a community group that wanted to convert it into a secondary school, and the Independent Development Trust and DET had agreed to help. In line with Eskom's policy of giving community groups responsibility for projects, the group was supposed to form a trust to take over the building.

One year later neither the community nor other participants had taken action. Meanwhile, the building had been vandalised and Eskom threatened to take it back. The threat prompted action: the community arranged for students at another school to "squat" in it, and then organised the trust. Although a year had been lost and damage done, the project got back on track.

The successes also add up — mainly the electrification of more than 400 schools since 1992, when Eskom embarked on an aggressive programme. This process will accelerate: Eskom plans to electrify 400 schools in 1995, focusing on older schools. 'If you make someone literate and provide water and electricity, we can pull out of our problem in South Africa,' suggests Cohn.

Besides electrification, Cohn is proud of Eskom's support to PROMAT College's teacher in-service development programmes that train teachers from rural areas. Eskom covers two-thirds of course costs. Participation has grown steadily and includes teachers who register a second time to upgrade their skills. The programme, based in Cullinan near Pretoria, has added satellite campuses in Durban, KaNgwane and Secunda.

Creative strategies

Cohn comments that future CSI planning at Eskom is contingent on foreign investment as well as the government's plans regarding the RDP, which had not been announced at the time of our interview. If, for example, foreign funds are funnelled into infrastructure development, Eskom might change its focus.

Cohn is especially concerned about the role that companies can, and she thinks should, take in regions that have been ignored. Citing Transkei as an example, she points to opportunities to develop the areas coastline. Few businesses had a presence there in the past, but Eskom is now taking over the supply of electricity in formerly self-governing territories and the former TVBC states, and is therefore beginning to get involved with community development projects in these areas.

Cohn proposes a solution that would enable NGOs already working in the Transkei to become its development partners, as Eskom is doing elsewhere in South Africa. And she is 'amazingly optimistic' about the potential for projects and for CSI in general to have enormous impact in South Africa's redevelopment.

Gencor Development Trust
PO Box 61820
Marshalltown 2017
Phone: (011) 376-2125
Fax: (011) 376-2458

Summary:
The Gencor Development Trust has evolved into a hands-on CSI programme that focuses on the community development process or ongoing programmes rather than specific projects, with a current emphasis on entrepreneurship training. This process entails extensive networking between the Trust, community groups, employees when the projects are based in areas where they live, NGOs, parastatals, and, often, other corporate partners. The Trust has a full-time staff of 11, including specialists in small business development, job creation and skill training, and education. As the result of unbundling by the parent company, the Trust has had to face budget cuts and the prospect of reducing staff. This dilemma has prompted a re-evaluation of the best way to use limited resources. The current solution is for each company in the Gencor group to form a CSI committee while the Trust manages programmes.

* * *

The Gencor Development Trust (GDT) has taken the "journey" from being a donations fund to a hands-on quasi-development agency — a trend its executive chairman, Kobus Visagie, says is likely to continue among larger firms to meet guidelines of the RDP.

Gencor's CSI is significant for a number of reasons. First, Visagie has long been active in promoting CSI networking; he spearheaded the formation of SAGA, the association of grantmakers. Second, he has ardently promoted the importance of CSI as a business function. Third, Gencor itself, prior to the unbundling of some of its subsidiary firms in 1993, was among South Africa's largest corporate donors. After the unbundling, the Trust was left with fewer resources but continued to sponsor major development projects, increasingly in partnership with other companies and sometimes with government or foreign donors. (Visagie travels once a year to Europe to visit prospective funding partners.) In this respect, the GDT is an interesting case study of how a CSI programme adapts when the parent company spins off some of its units.

Background

Gencor's giving programme started about 25 years ago as a chairman's donations fund. By 1984 it had grown large enough to warrant formation of a trust to enable the company to get tax relief for its gifts. There are actually two trusts — one for education and one for social welfare. Visagie was hired to run it 1988.

Under Visagie, who has a background in education and agricultural development, GDT spends about half of its budget, after overheads are deducted, on proactive, on-the-ground development. This approach conforms with his belief that CSI should serve as 'an attempt to assist in the creation of a socio-economic and sociopolitical environment conductive to real economic growth. It has the same goals as most members of civil society, to do these things without violence, and with education, housing and other services,' he says. 'But I always have to tell my board that it's also good for business, not just for their conscience.' Besides himself, his staff includes four senior managers, one administrative clerk, one administrative/finance manager, three secretaries and one part-time field officer who visits projects.

The CSI budget is set according to a percentage of dividends declared from Gencor companies, usually about 1,3 percent. Visagie keeps 10 percent of the total for management and administrative costs and another small portion for joint ventures with institutions such as the Urban Foundation and for grants to tertiary institutions that are part of the standard donations programme. Major gifts are decided by the GDT's board of trustees, who at this writing were all white men — executive chairmen at each of the Gencor companies — although Visagie was in the process of recruiting black board members.

In addition, each of Gencor's units has development committees known as Employee-Community Support Groups, some with lower-level supervisory and management employees as well as trade union members; Visagie's office helps administer these committees. They assist community groups in developing project proposals and then choose the best for funding. The budget itself is centralised and all cheques come through this office. After administrative overheads are deducted, GDT's funds are divided between donations and hands-on programmes.

GDT's final full-year budget before the unbundling was R16,5 million, which Visagie expected would drop by about 40 percent when all implications of the unbundling were final. As required by law, GDT maintains audited statements which are available to public on request. Visagie supports full disclosure and hopes the new government will make it compulsory. In 1994, the Trust launched *GDT Mirror*, an in-house newsletter, to describe its activities to employees.

Joint ventures

Gencor is among a growing number of companies involved in joint ventures. With Eskom as a regular partner (and in conjunction with the DET), the Trust is working on 15 school-building projects costing an average of R4 million each. These are planned as community schools in which Gencor is project facilitator, the schools ministry invests state funds and local labour undertakes the construction. A key aspect of the programme is that it achieves many things at once: it builds capacity within the community, since community-based building committees decide how the school will be used, what it should look like and who should be employed; it taps government funds in a "user-friendly" fashion; it regards the community as "owners" of the project; and it creates jobs. Each GDT manager has a role to play: Pierre Lourens coordinates the job creation component; Louis Pretorius oversees small business development; and Eric Ratshikhopha supervises the education part.

GDT likes to see itself as programme- rather than project-oriented. For instance, the 1992 programme emphasis was on social infrastructure and capacity building, the 1993 focus on the construction of schools and community centres, and the objectives for 1994 were on entrepreneurship development. This doesn't mean that an earlier theme is abandoned; rather, each new emphasis is an outgrowth of the previous year's work. By year-end 1993, Gencor had identified six regions with well-developed community structures, but a next step was still to be accomplished: the creation of an entrepreneurship facility to develop jobs, literacy and skills training. Local mines need a source for nuts and bolts, and the Entrepreneurship Development Centre (EDC), modelled on the SBDC small business "hives", would identify someone to manufacture and supply them. A hive is a large facility that provides workspaces for new businesses, and offers access to telephones, electricity and other services at discounted rates. The EDCs link needs with resources as they provide facilities and opportunities for new entrepreneurs.

In 1994, GDT's schools programme emphasised creating support systems for principals and department heads in the form of new resource centres and the upgrading of existing training facilities with computers. Such a project often involves collaborating with an NGO, such as READ, that has long experience in the field.

A concrete strategy to bring CSI in line with the RDP

The GDT's new planning strategies incorporate RDP guidelines by taking into account the socio-economic needs of Gencor employee communities with available resources, such as facilities at closed mines that can be recycled for other use. Pierre Lourens, Manager: Programmes, who specialises in community development and reconstruction, engages in what he calls 'dialogical interventions' to encourage communities to change their preconceptions of how projects work. He then tries to develop a showcase project. 'People need to see results,' he says. 'My aim *isn't* school building per se but people development and economic empowerment.' To implement his plan, he brings four stakeholders together: schools, communities, NGOs (trainers) and the private sector.

It isn't easy. For one thing, until the 1994 changeover in government, communities often rejected input of the schools departments because they were seen to be "illegitimate" outgrowths of apartheid. Second, the communities themselves often lacked the resources of capital and knowledge to become active "players" in the project. Too often 'they only see themselves as recipients', Lourens explained. 'I had to get them to see themselves as resources.' And, third, it was necessary to add strong support structures to the equation, mainly trainers who could train unskilled, unqualified community residents to have a useful role in projects. To this end, Lourens works with trainers from construction firms such as Murray & Roberts or Stocks & Stocks to manage community participation.

In past instances, GDT would then sign an agreement with the DET stating that if the schools department would pay 75 percent of the cost of the school, the Trust would raise the balance from the private sector and oversee the community involvement process. Key to ensuring that this process works is keeping the community involved. When all is done, 'It's "win-win" for everyone,' notes Lourens. 'The DET saves money, we create jobs and goodwill, and a school is available to the community.'

But while most projects are 'win-win', some do fail. Visagie recalls how, after 18 meetings with a community that was lobbying for a new school and getting the necessary mandates to proceed, the community committee finally pulled out. 'They expected to get more money after April 27 [1994],' said Visagie, who was first interviewed before the election. 'The realities are going to be very different.'

Within communities, expectations are often high and projects do not always work out as planned. But they can proceed as long as there are 'small victories' and have community input. But who are these communities? 'We don't define them as Soweto or Alexandra but as small groups of doers within them — people who depend on each other for economic survival,' points out Visagie. 'They include town councils, engineers, welfare workers, ministers, etc. This approach ensures access to all available resources — organisation, expertise, facilities and capital.'

Requests are overwhelming

In 1993, Visagie's offices received almost 19 000 funding appeals. There is no form to fill in; the Trust reviews all as long as they contain a budget, plans and a description of the applicant's track record. The appeals are divided between the staff for initial review. 'Most applications are of high quality, and they're getting better, I think, because of better training from SAIF [South African Institute of Fund Raising], UNISA, etc.,' Visagie says. 'The best salesmen usually get the most money, even though they don't always represent the best projects. So sometimes employees are a good source of information, and we also get information through the CSI network.' But as budgets grow tight and needs greater, donors are becoming more choosy, Visagie finds. 'The South African market is getting much more sophisticated.' The Trust prefers to make fewer, but larger, grants to large groups because it feels these will go further.

'The most complicated, diversified job you can have'

Anyone who meets Kobus Visagie is likely to leave exhausted. He seems to speak twice as fast as the average South African and do twice as much. Despite the job's demands, he clearly loves it. 'CSI is the most complicated, diversified and exciting job you can have,' he says. 'It gives you the ability to be creative and function on many levels and in many disciplines. You must be able to deal with variety, do many things at once, be versatile and innovative, and have good analytic skills.'

Visagie started as a teacher of agriculture and then got involved in farmworker training in Potchefstroom. He has an honours degree in industrial psychology and a master's degree in strategic management. Before joining Gencor, he spent six years at the Development Bank of Southern Africa. He got his current job through a newspaper advert, 'when I needed to get out of bureaucracy of a parastatal,' he says.

These days Visagie acknowledges that someone with his energy and vision — and background — would probably not get the job because of an emphasis on affirmative action. But at Gencor, he says, he hasn't been artificially pressurised to hire blacks. Two of his four senior managers are black and the field officer is a black woman.

Visagie believes that few of South Africa's 'captains of industry fully appreciate the scope of what we do', principally because a CSI department is not a profit centre. Without this support, the potential for physical and psychological burnout is high.

Even so, Visagie wouldn't do anything else. CSI 'will be the most exciting field to be in for the next 10 to 15 years in South Africa; it's doing development that keeps the adrenaline flowing. But our challenge is to stay legitimate, and companies need to recognise the importance and professionalism of CSI managers.'

Johannesburg Consolidated Investment Company, Limited
PO Box 590
Johannesburg 2000
Phone: (011) 373-9111
Fax: (011) 834-5065

Summary:

Although JCI has to date maintained a low CSI profile, its pro-gramme ranks in size with companies like Gencor and Nedcor, and it is much admired within the CSI community both for its own ini-tiatives and its many partnerships with other companies. JCI was the only company in this study to indicate that top executives recognise the essential role CSI can play in shaping the group's response to the RDP. One of the CSI department's two managers sits on an industry public policy committee and plays a role in public policy as well as human resources issues. One of JCI's major CSI initiatives is its Group Education and Development Unit (GEDU), a programme at a number of "adopted" schools which provides in-service training for teachers; upgrading of student skills in science, technical and administrative areas for which JCI would anticipate a need for employees; and improvement of school laboratories and other key facilities and infrastructures. The current restructuring process will see the JCI Group split into three new companies, and while the pre-cise CSI policies of the new entities are unclear at the time of writing, all three have committed to themselves to a CSI programme.

*   *   *

Johannesburg Consolidated Investment Company Limited — JCI for short (and sometimes known by its nickname "Johnnies") — has kept a low CSI profile. Yet within the corporate donor commu-nity, its programmes are well known and respected. This is perhaps because CSI manager Caroline Tindall — who prefers to keep out of the spotlight — has one of the longest and most consistent track records in a profession which is still finding its way, and she knows her constituencies well. JCI's CSI team balances high-impact pro-grammes and support for national initiatives with smaller projects to help communities in areas where the group has operations or recruits employees (mainly the former homelands of Transkei and Ciskei). The company prefers the term involvement to investment, because its projects entail more than financial input; dealing in a conservative industry requires greater hands-on engagement in order to make projects happen.

This approach is a far cry from the early days, when JCI founder Barney Barnato funded charity projects which were the epitome of a Victorian paternalism. For decades following, as at most other companies, social spending was a "peripheral" activity handled by the company secretary.

Tindall joined the company in the late 1970s and assisted in the group's employee housing-purchase programme, which was formed after the 1976 unrest in Soweto. This was a time when many companies were assessing their community obligations: the Anglo American and De Beers Chairman's Fund was just two years old and the Urban Foundation was getting off the ground. As Tindall puts it, she gradually "slid" into the management of JCI's donations programme. Bringing organisational skills she had honed as an assistant to several Progressive Federal Party MPs in Parliament earlier in the decade, she helped turn a conventional donations programme into what she dubs "appropriate" funding through an on-the-ground approach and a close working relationship with grantees. 'We don't talk about donations — anyone can make donations — we're *plugged* into our projects,' she points out. JCI's CSI maintains a flexibility that Tindall regards as crucial to a successful programme: 'We have few rigid areas (for example, we don't fund individuals), so we can respond to community needs.'

Furthermore, as the demands of the RDP take on more urgency, key top people are getting involved, including managers and engineers who, says Tindall, are becoming more sensitised to social needs that they would previously have ignored. This is important for a diversified firm with some 60 000 employees: a large, multi-faceted group of companies, JCI has various "managed" operations, which include finance, mining and property holdings, and an investment side with holdings in many other companies. Its CSI applies to the managed companies within JCI.

Nowadays, as the programme has grown and become more proactive, Tindall shares a heavy workload with co-manager Marc Gonsalves, two project officers and one administrative officer — and they still don't have enough time for their work. Gonsalves is a former Marist Brother with a background in education who joined JCI in 1990 after he left the order, to work as senior education officer in the JCI's Group Education and Development Unit (GEDU). He later moved into human resources training and in 1992 joined the CSI Department.

Making the link between policy and CSI

A fascinating feature of JCI's CSI is the extent to which it is linked with public policy initiatives. Working under the Group's Strategy and Public Affairs Consultant, Dr Nick Segal, the CSI team reports directly to the group's Administrative Committee, composed of the Group Chairman and four other senior directors, and not through human resources or marketing. As a result, the CSI programme's insights and experiences are shared directly with top managers, who tend to be active in key national business initiatives. A number of JCI executives are involved in public policy issues through the Chamber of Mines, the Consultative Business Movement (CBM), the former National Economic Forum and Business South Africa. Some were on the corporate team that talked to the ANC prior to its unbanning.

An interesting aspect of JCI's CSI is its willingness to help projects instigated by other firms that bring it little publicity. 'We've sometimes given the "topping off" costs,'Tindall explains. 'We've kept a low profile because of our low consumer base, but we know we need to raise it.' When Eunice Sibiya of Coca-Cola South Africa needed R29 000 for a school-building project at Zonkisizwe informal settlement, JCI was able to respond.

A no-disclosure policy — for now

JCI would not divulge its social spending budget, in accordance with a current policy not to make such data public. Tindall and Gonsalves agree that the company should (and, they believe, will) become more transparent, in line with an overall trend among companies. They would say only that JCI's CSI spending is roughly even with Gencor's and Nedcor's, which means that it hovers between R8 million and R15 million per year (it can fluctuate depending on the price of platinum and gold). JCI's plans to raise its profile won't end the partnerships with other companies but means that the company will seek more credit.

As with a number of other companies, JCI's budget is divided between a chairman's fund, for general projects, and a chairman's fund educational trust, which funds tax-exempt educational projects. The programme funds three general areas: 1) national initiatives that have direct impact on the company, such as CBM, the Joint Education Trust, the SBDC and tertiary institutions (about 50 percent of the budget); 2) projects that represent "strategic self-interest" to JCI, including, for example, GEDU's adopted schools and literacy projects which have spin-offs for the company's human resources division by serving communities where JCI has operations (30 to 40 percent of CSI spending); and 3) general charitable projects (welfare organisations and community, educational or cultural projects that offer no benefit to the company). This last area has grown in importance in the past two years, and spending has risen from 11 percent of the budget to 19 percent.

A policy of consistency

In all JCI funds about 1 500 organisations, many of which regularly receive some form of support. 'We're committed to ongoing support,' says Tindall, although a portion of the budget is allocated for new projects. The department will "warn" projects when their funding might be discontinued, but Tindall believes strongly in staying with projects that JCI has helped to develop. But she also dislikes the prospect of an NGO becoming too donor-dependent. Organisations with a solid infrastructure and national impact, such as READ and SEP, get ongoing support, but JCI scrupulously tracks how their programmes change and adjusts donations accordingly.

On the complex and time-consuming monitoring and evaluation side, Tindall admits that JCI comes up short. 'We just don't have enough capacity, so we depend on report-backs, and project officers do some site visits,' she says. Since JCI does much of its funding in partnerships, it has not experienced many failures on its own.

One project which JCI helped launch but has had a mixed record is Phuthing School, a non-racial school near Woodmead formed prior to the unbanning of the ANC. Part of the New Era Schools Trust, Phuthing ran into a funding crunch after 1990 when some of its funders turned their support to new types of projects, such as those catering for returned exiles. JCI helped to build the school, seconded personnel to assist with finances and marketing, placed corporate members on its board and committees, and helped get it back on its feet. These days it has a science and technology centre and a pre-primary programme as well as a high school and an outreach programme into the community.

GEDU

A centrepiece of JCI's CSI is the Group Education and Development Unit (GEDU), a programme formed in 1990 which operates in some 30 pre-primary, primary and secondary schools in and around the JCI Group's areas of operation. GEDU provides in-service training for teachers in maths, science and English, upgrading of student skills, library management, career guidance, and entrepreneurship and management training for principals. It also invests in school laboratories and infrastructure (including classrooms, libraries, toilets and administration offices) plus educational equipment and resources (ranging from typewriters and generators to specific educational programmes such as Breakthrough to Literacy). Based in James Park, JCI's Group training centre in Randfontein, it is staffed by 11 education/training officers, some of whom also work on the company's Adult Basic Education and Training initiatives.

Lack of capacity is made up for with a lot of heart

One consequence of JCI's low profile on CSI is a low awareness of its existence among employees, including managers concerned with bottom-line issues. (JCI's CSI has only recently begun to be publicised in-house through an employee newsletter called *Newslink*.) So gratification often has to come from satisfaction in the work itself. 'You have to have a heart to do this kind of work,' asserts Tindall. 'This is something Marc and I have often talked about.' Such empathy, as well as seeing the fruits of their work, makes up somewhat for the lack of capacity.

In addition, Tindall and Gonsalves have seen their work rise in importance because of its growing relevance, particularly with the onset of the RDP. 'It's not just us and how we work with NGOs, it's also how we understand the civics and local government,' Tindall explains. Through their work, she and Gonsalves have contact with a wide spectrum of organisations which are resources for the group. Gonsalves sits on the Public Policy Advisory Committee at the Chamber of Mines.

It's not always smooth-going, and Tindall notes that endurance and flexibility are among the main qualities that a person in her position needs. 'You have to be a bit of everything, which is why it's good to have several people in the department. We come from different backgrounds, and there's a creative tension and we serve as devil's advocate to each other,' she says. 'And it is sometimes necessary to disagree with the directors on a programme, and having a staff to back you up makes a big difference.'

"The most incredible field to be in"

Despite the drawbacks, Tindall considers CSI to be 'the most incredible field to be in'. Marc Gonsalves concurs: 'You straddle the most interesting mix of people,' he says. 'The real heartbeat comes from seeing people on the ground, especially women', of whom, he adds: 'they give me more confidence in the likely success of a project when they're on a committee'.

In addition, they've observed how some peoples' attitudes have changed. In one instance, the company inherited mineral rights on a farm and decided to renovate a local house into a school for children in the community. Doing the job required an interface between the company, workers and the community, which is an ideal way to develop a project and a good RDP strategy. A team from the mine upgraded the house, and a variety of local new partnerships were formed; a church group knitted jerseys for the children; programmes of "non-formal education" for adults were offered, and the GEDU team came in.

Such creative use of existing spaces is important, as is the input of education bridging programmes which JCI supports. These range from the Rhodes University-based Molteno Project to universities and technikons nationwide.

Liberty Life Foundation
PO Box 10499
Johannesburg 2000
Phone: (011) 408-3298
Fax: (011) 408-3998

Summary:

Since it was launched in 1990 with an aggressive five-year, R100 million social investment budget, the Liberty Life Foundation has developed a high profile as one of South Africa's most proactive corporate philanthropies. It has shown an unusual willingness to support new organisations with good leadership, a sound structure and a long-term plan even though they may not yet have a track record, and to fund areas, such as AIDS and HIV education and prevention, that other corporate donors shy away from. In 1994, the Liberty Life Group Community Fund announced a matching grants programme — possibly the first of its kind by a South African-owned company — which encourages employees to make donations to accredited non-profit organisations by matching that grant. Excluding spending on marketing and internal HR development, the Liberty Life Foundation is South Africa's second largest corporate philanthropy.

*   *   *

If there's one term to describe the Liberty Life Foundation, it's "hands-on". An autonomous corporate philanthropy formed in 1990 as the consolidation of four funds, it has grown rapidly since the company announced a R100 million, five-year programme to focus on education and development.

To manage such a large budget and programme, the Foundation has a full-time staff of 12 headed by Executive Trustee Hylton Appelbaum, the son-in-law of Liberty Life's founder, Donald Gordon, and an Executive Director of Liberty Life who also serves on the board of the Kagiso Trust. Its two principal grant officers spend much of their time in the field and are backed up by a full-time writer/administrator who attends to the writing and project motivations which the grant officers do not have time to prepare. An ample clerical staff support the development work of the foundation. Many of their tasks, in addition to site visits, are often done singlehandedly by CSI personnel at other companies, a situation some say hinders their effectiveness. As more companies adopt RDP guidelines as part of their social investment agendas, some, such as Gencor and Nedcor, have also created a staff structure with field officers and in-house support.

This is not to say that such support makes life easy for Liberty Life's project officers; each is responsible for up to 100 projects, and their involvement is time-consuming and often emotionally draining. 'You can't be a development person and funder at the same time,' says project officer Hugh McLean, who has been with the Foundation since its start and provided most of the information for this profile. (Author's note: the Liberty Life Foundation provided a grant to help with this project.)

Liberty Life's path-finding approach resulted from what McLean describes as the failure of attempts by the company in 1989 and 1990 to engage some of its counterparts in a national development collaboration to promote social change. This may have been a function of the times: a simultaneous effort by Gencor's Kobus Visagie to launch a national CSI network also fell through, although he and a few dozen CSI professionals, including Appelbaum and McLean, met regularly to share ideas. So Donald Gordon announced the creation of the Liberty Life Foundation and challenged other companies to follow suit.

(In 1991, a number of South Africa's largest companies formed the financial core of the JET, a project which also brought in trade unions and a wide spectrum of political groups to 'kick-start' adult basic education, teacher upgrading and projects for marginalised youth. And in 1994, Kobus Visagie got his wish when the grant-makers association, SAGA was formed; Liberty Life Foundation is a charter member and McLean was elected to its first board and is its treasurer.)

The Foundation includes the Liberty Life Group Community Fund, formed in 1983, and the Donald Gordon Foundation, a private charitable trust established in the 1960s. Despite some differentiation between them, their finances are consolidated in an annual report which lists all grant recipients as well as the sum allocated per category.

From the outset, the Liberty Life Foundation already perceived its role to be developmental rather than donations-based. 'We tend to think of CSI as corporate social *involvement* as opposed to investment, because of our partnerships — a shift of business into the development terrain, rather than the other way around,' says McLean, who taught in Bophuthatswana for some years and speaks a workable Setswana and Zulu.

Moreover, the project officers are allowed considerable leeway in their work, a situation which McLean believes is unusual. Some foundations take their direction from a single personality, but the Liberty Life Foundation does not have a single unified view. 'I have one, the trustees have one, and Hylton Appelbaum has one,' notes McLean.

Transparency

The 1993 annual report is fairly thorough and discloses more about its CSI spending than most companies do. It lists all organisations that received funds from 1990 through 1993, divided into four broad categories — education, social transformation, social intervention and development — which are arranged into 42 subcategories, ranging from traditional welfare organisations to grassroots development groups and the alternative media. Within the education category, the highest priority is early childhood development, including existing centres and agencies, children's media and support for a national educare body.

More recent efforts have been made to support innovative programmes for children who lack access to quality educare, mainly in rural areas. These include programmes that help mothers improve their children's nutrition and basic education. The Foundation continues to support adult basic education, community programmes, technikons, universities, teacher training projects and education policy development.

In a few instances, the Foundation has made huge grants, as in the case of its R18 million gift to the School of Public and Development Management (P&DM) at the University of the Witwatersrand. Affiliated with the Wits University School of Business, P&DM is headquartered in the new Donald Gordon Building.

Matching gifts

In a separate initiative to encourage a culture of giving, the Liberty Life Group Community Fund, drawing on US models, introduced a matching gifts scheme in 1994 in which the company equals on a one-to-one basis employee donations. These may range from R25 to R2 000 to charitable, non-governmental, civic and other organisations. The gifts can be in the form of cash, shares or property. Matching gifts will not be made to organisations that have exclusionary clauses; private clubs or organisations; religious organisations that do not also provide a social service; sports promotion; other groups that fundraise; foreign organisations whose mission does not help South Africa; and individuals. These guidelines are spelled out in a brochure available to all employees. (Actually, individual giving is already the major source of philanthropy in South Africa, according to a 1990 study of national giving patterns by Business & Marketing Intelligence.)

As with most other corporate foundations, the Liberty Life Foundation is swamped with proposals. Those seeking up to R20 000 may be approved for funding through the Liberty Life Community Fund and do not require trustee approval. Larger sums must be agreed by the trustees, who meet bi-monthly. Most grants range from R30 000 to R100 000.

Too involved?

There can be real problems — and losses — in becoming too hands-on if projects are not adequately supervised. McLean learned this lesson the hard way. The Foundation had agreed to support a computer training programme that had many computers but, ultimately, no trainees. 'It looked interesting on paper, and the project director told me she had promises of support from US AID [US Agency for International Development], Kagiso Trust and the IDT [Independent Development Trust].' Based on her claims and agreeing with the programme's structure and goals, Liberty Life committed a substantial sum. Months later, when no training had begun while its highly paid staff continued to grow (including the appointment to key jobs of relatives of the programme director), McLean called for an overhaul of the project plus full disclosure. Funding was put on hold.

The Foundation then faced two alternatives, McLean says: to 'completely formalise our relations, withdraw into a donor cocoon and keep our hands off' — or remain hands-on but monitor grants more closely and not release the full amount right away. Liberty Life chose the latter. This procedure requires grantees to sign contracts with the Foundation and file monthly claims requesting a fixed amount and explaining how it will be used. They can claim large amounts early in the funding cycle, but the Foundation keeps a careful watch to make sure funds are not abused. The new system takes more time, but forces the grantee to be more accountable.

Redefining success

Defining success is one of the most difficult issues facing CSI managers. A pitfall of many CSI projects is that both funders and grantees may have unrealistic — and quite different — expectations of a project's outcome. Over time McLean has often had to readjust his own assessments of what makes a project worthwhile.

'I tend to be more satisfied with modest successes,' he says. 'In the development field, small changes are often significant changes.' For instance, the Youth Development Programme (YDP), to which the Foundation gave R15 000 in seed money — the annual donation has since grown — cannot be easily assessed in absolute terms. YDP is a self-help group of about 18 Soweto youth between the ages of 19 and 24 who failed their matric and wanted to rewrite it and equip themselves with other skills that would enable them to find work or create their own jobs. (See project profile.) They do not have a regular office but meet regularly, have taken courses in basic computer skills, and, more important, in McLean's view, have persevered in improving themselves and creating a structure and discipline that gives them hope at a frustrating time in their lives.

Liberty Life's venture into educare support in rural areas is an example of how a project can be a success, a disaster and a learning experience all at once. The directors of an NGO which trained local women in teaching skills encountered problems which no one was prepared for. They found their students to be enthusiastic and rapid learners. But once empowered, some teachers started becoming what McLean calls 'high-heeled', and wore nice dresses to the school even though these were not appropriate for their work. The workshop exposure prompted them to begin seeking opportunities beyond the rural communities where they lived.

As the teachers became empowered, parents and local civics appeared jealous and even threatened by these women. The head of a local development committee refused to release funds for the educare centre. The jealousy sometimes turned into political conflict among community factions that wanted to preserve their power bases. Church leaders and tribal elders were pitted against ANC Youth League members. Making matters worse, the first group of teachers were from just one village, and villages not included showed their resentment. One community leader barred the NGO's trainees from his areas.

The programme succeeded by providing 12 well-trained community-based teachers for local pre-schools. But because the teachers did not get community support, no more than 20 children were enrolled in the pilot pre-school and very few benefited. And the teachers expected to be paid at a time when no money was coming in. It was a mess.

The Liberty Life Foundation still supports work in the area, but a new initiative will include more than one village and have more resources. The centre will take a more 'holistic' approach, with projects in nutrition and health, input from churches and civics as well as schools, and involvement of elders from the start. A key lesson from this experience is that educare must be far more than school preparation, but must address other needs of children growing up in poverty. Nutrition education, feeding schemes, vegetable gardens and projects that bring older relatives (for instance, to tell stories) and siblings (to help with learning-readiness) comprise an enriching approach that makes use of available resources.

Early days . . . and future plans

Hugh McLean was offered a job at the Liberty Life Foundation by Hylton Appelbaum just as it was starting out in 1990. What interested Appelbaum was McLean's background as an educator and community development worker with grassroots skills and a rapport with people. Based on his prior work, McLean was prepared for the mixed results of funded projects, although he has also learned on the job.

McLean is aware of the contradictions that arise when a funder becomes too involved in a project and recognises the need to keep a 'donor's distance'. 'You need a certain creative tension — to be hands-on *and* hands-off — keep your distance but also be accessible, friendly and critical.' In an effort to keep the creativity but also learn how to 'cost out development and obtain a more "managed" way to understand society', McLean has been studying for an MBA. Increasing practical business skills is a wise route for the CSI professional, particularly in a foundation that has already taken a maverick role in setting new standards for CSI.

The Lotus Trust
PO Box 4126
Rivonia 2128
Phone: (011) 884-5667
Fax: (011) 884-5890

Summary:

When US software manufacturer Lotus Development Corporation returned to South Africa in 1992 after divesting in the mid-1980s, it wanted to do so in a "politically correct" way. So, in addition to knocking on the right political doors just before launching operations, the company announced the formation of a social investment trust that would support grassroots training groups — preferably black-run — by providing software, some computer hardware and the technical expertise needed to get them working. In line with his theme of "change, not charity" — and in tandem with Lotus's own goals — Trust director Mackie McLeod, an African-American with an activist background, has sought out groups that empower people to become self-sufficient. In addition, Lotus sponsors an internship programme that trains people in computer skills and helps place them in jobs. Since 1992, the Lotus Trust has provided black-led South African NGOs and community-based organisations with cash grants amounting to approximately US $300 000.

*   *   *

If there's anything that sums up Mackie McLeod's approach to running the Lotus Trust, it's the idea of self-sufficiency. 'The new South Africa will be heavily dependent on national, not international, donors,' he says. 'South Africa has to pick up its own tab.'

To that end, in his role as the first Executive Director of the Trust, the Sandton-based philanthropic arm of software company Lotus Development Corporation, McLeod has attempted to develop partnerships with local firms and obtain matching funds from other donors to stretch resources. The main problem, he says, is that good partners have been hard to find and the matching fund programme, when we spoke, was not yet off the ground. (However, talks were under way with California-based Silicon Graphics International, a new entrant to South Africa, about forming a technology training consortium initiated by the Trust.)

'The distance between conversation and action is vast here, and very little is being done. People feel threatened,' McLeod says.

'Those not willing to subscribe to "change not charity" are finding volumes of excuses why not to act. So at a time when the pie should be growing, there's *no* corresponding increase in funding to meet local needs.' This may seem like an overreaction, but McLeod comes from an aggressively more activist background than most of his local counterparts profiled in this book.

An African-American from Boston, Massachusetts, McLeod was involved in many grassroots and international social movements, including anti-apartheid work, before he moved to Zimbabwe in 1990 to work on development projects sponsored by the American Friends Service Committee. He was recruited by Lotus in 1991 when the company embarked on plans to return to South Africa.

A long Lotus connection

McLeod's acquaintance with Lotus predates his arrival in Southern Africa. The company was founded in 1982 in Cambridge, Massachusetts, by a group of politically active 'baby boomers' and computer hackers, and the firm launched a philanthropic programme two years later. Even then, Lotus's philosophy of giving was well-defined: to make technology and training available to people with the least access to it. A key reason for this originated at the home office; although Lotus's headquarters were located in a depressed area outside Boston, its employees were recruited primarily from elite universities, and some became quite wealthy from the business while still quite young; few local residents qualified for jobs at the company.

So the Lotus Philanthropy Programme, which eventually became a fully-fledged department with five people at headquarters and 12 offices worldwide, developed the theme of 'change not charity' — a phrase McLeod repeated several times in our interview. As part of the Lotus international programme, the Trust follows basic global guidelines which encourage local communities to take control of their destinies through training that gives them skills to become competitive in the marketplace. As part of this process, Lotus South Africa prefers to fund black-led groups to encourage empowerment.

Although Lotus had operations in South Africa in the 1980s, it closed its offices during the sanctions era and only returned in early 1992. Like most other US software firms in South Africa, its operations focus on marketing and product support, and Lotus Development South Africa has just 30 employees, with no plans for major expansion. Its CSI budget is therefore modest — it was launched with a R1 million grant from its parent in 1992.

The amount is usually tied to 1 percent of pretax profits, although as the value of the rand has fallen, McLeod has pressed for more. Even so, he had not spent the full amount by mid-1994, since he needed several months of groundwork and site visits before he could start making grants. (Adding its donations of software and hardware, the value of Lotus's philanthropy comes closer to 2,5 percent of pretax profits.) Some R400 000 was distributed in 1992 and the remaining R600 000 was rolled over for 1993 and into 1994.

Election-related funding was substantial: R150 000 for voter education to Matla Trust and the Southern Africa project run by the Washington-based Lawyers' Committee for Civil Rights Under Law. Lotus's headquarters office donated US $50 000 to the South African Fund for Free Elections.

Lotus's 1994 priorities reflect a targeted approach typical of small US companies, with a focus on women's empowerment, education and health. The Trust gave R30 000 in software and hardware to help the Women's National Coalition run a study on women's needs and funded the Women's Development Foundation to train women to run for election.

The largest recipients since the Trust began operating have been training organisations: the African Institute of Technology (AIT) (see page 147), the Community Education Computer Society and Zakheni Computing each received R75 000 in 1992. South African Non-Governmental Organisation Network (SANGONet), the electronic bulletin board created by the Development Resources Centre, received R50 000.

Creating internships: A CSI innovation

A creative component of Lotus's CSI is its six-month internship programme, which identifies talented black students, trains them in computer skills and places them in NGOs or companies as interns. The Trust pays the intern a monthly stipend of R1 500, plus R600 for transport. Participating companies have included Edgar's, Old Mutual, the Soft Sheen International Foundation, South African Airways, South African Rail Commuter Corporation, WordPerfect South Africa and Lotus itself.

The programme offers basic and more advanced computer skills, depending on the intern's background (some participants have been returned exiles with good skills who could not find work), and training in interpersonal communication and other skills to adapt to a corporate ambiance. This programme is directed by

Jonatheen Beyers, the Trust's Human Resources Development Manager and a member of its board.

In a separate programme, Lotus has given bursaries to talented black computer trainers and to attend two-week "train-the-trainer" workshops at Lotus's Cambridge headquarters to learn the company's newest software and teach its use in South Africa. There's an obvious profit motive here — it promotes the desirability of using Lotus software — while giving cutting-edge skills to black trainers.

Full disclosure

In keeping with Lotus's disclosure policy, McLeod has assembled the company's first annual review, covering its first two years of operation. Entitled 'Building Tomorrow's South Africa Today', the 34-page report lists all grantees and monies disbursed and descriptions of a few. About 75 percent of donations are the result of direct requests, mostly by fax or mail. McLeod and his staff evaluate them according to pre-set guidelines (which Lotus sends on request).

Applicants must be a state-registered NGO or CBO or be able to receive funds through another registered organisation and fill out a standardised form. Then Lotus staff do site visits to assess the worthiness of projects, and make further visits as part of a checking process. Recipients must file quarterly reports of two to five pages which describe how the funding has been used and to ensure that the guidelines have been adhered to.

Future plans

In 1995 the Trust plans to launch a training and technology demonstration project, Foundation for Applied Information Technology (FAIT). FAIT is a micro-enterprise that aims to offer high-level, company-authorised training to CBOs and to small and medium-sized businesses as an in-kind contribution to black South African community development. Its clients would come from civics, clinics, multiracial educational institutions and women's training and development organisations.

FAIT will emphasise using computer networks as organisational tools to disseminate information; it will subsidise clients who cannot pay, while those who can will be charged a nominal fee. FAIT's operating overhead will be drawn from a donor consortium that McLeod is organising.

McLeod has met with such foreign donors as the International Development Research Centre (in Canada), Finn-Aid, and Swedish and Norwegian groups that remain involved in South Africa, as prospective partners in this effort. 'Their sensibilities are very different, and we can learn from Interfund [a Johannesburg-based agency that channels Scandinavian and Canadian funds into South Africa],' he finds.

In addition, McLeod remains involved with US organisations that provide financial and material aid to grassroots groups in South Africa, such as Boston-based Fund for a Free South Africa and Tecschange, which offers technical support and hardware and software to needy groups.

On a local level, the Lotus Trust plans to support projects in the Pietermaritzburg-Durban area and the Cape Flats that provide training and computer facilities. The Trust would help convert unused community centres into computer labs which can double as training facilities. In addition, Lotus will hold more "show-and-tell" events to demonstrate development-oriented applications of information technology at technikons, universities and other organisations that promote it. (This activity also serves to promote the use and sales of Lotus software.)

To date, McLeod reports no major failures among projects although many are threatened by the shift of donor resources from NGOs to the implementing structures of the RDP. Meanwhile, he finds national and international firms reluctant to replace what he calls 'well-meaning rhetoric' with a commitment to capacity- and skills-building projects and micro-enterprises for black South Africans.

'Most South African donors are for a disempowering philosophy,' he asserts. 'They'd rather focus on something like Red Nose Day, a one-day-a-year effort borrowed from the Brits. A handful of corporates and individuals within them' — he cites Premier and AECI as examples — 'subscribe to a broader vision than charity for the needy, but these are the exceptions to the rule'.

Despite his disappointments, McLeod reports 'no burnout at all, because there's a big window of opportunity to create new models', he says. 'This period has never been better to inspire people even if the recent past has not been inspiring.'

At year-end 1994 McLeod announced plans to leave the Lotus Trust; he had always intended to stay for several years to "kick-start" it and then turn it over to South African leadership. His deputy, Jonatheen Beyers, will direct the Trust while McLeod remains in Southern Africa as a technology consultant.

Murray & Roberts
PO Box 1000
Bedfordview 2008
Phone: (011) 455-1410
Fax: (011) 455-1322

Summary:

In some respects, CSI at the Murray & Roberts group of companies operates in a relatively conventional top-down manner, with minimal employee input. However, the size and nature of its CSI, its potential application to the Reconstruction and Development Programme through partnerships with its construction companies, and the group's strong emphasis on communication and a system of "core values", make its community participation worth exploring. Furthermore, Murray & Roberts' sponsorship of the Sunflower Projects, a hybrid of training and the profit motive (although it was reorganised into a not-for-gain company in 1993), is an interesting example of how a company can use its expertise to create an organisation that is socially responsible and also promotes the corporate image. Labour Research Service, which researches the social records of companies for the union-run Community Growth Fund unit trust, lists Murray & Roberts among the most progressive companies in its portfolio for its workplace policies.

*   *   *

Murray & Roberts' CSI programme at a group level appears conventional by the standards of this guide. Principal decisions are made by the Murray & Roberts Foundation, which receives 5 percent of group dividends for CSI spending, and remains a top-down process driven by the company's Commercial Director, Jeremy Ractliffe. Day-to-day CSI administration is handled by the public relations office, with one person assigned to it. But it is Ractliffe, and not the staff member, who is publicly associated with the company's CSI. The corporate communications department coordinates information on foundation activities throughout the group and externally.

The foundation's six board members include five group executives and Willie Esterhuyse, a non-executive director who is professor of ethics at Stellenbosch. They meet three times a year to make grant decisions. Policy guidelines favour projects that focus on "people-centred" development, a willingness to work in joint ventures with other corporate donors, and full disclosure to employees and the public. The Foundation seeks to support projects that can become self-sustaining.

But Murray & Roberts appears to be aware of the need to change its culture, and although its CSI may seem old-fashioned compared to most of the other companies discussed in this book, its mind-set is clearly enlightened. For instance, workers are elected to Murray & Roberts' housing committee to decide on how employee housing funds are to be allocated, and Ractliffe is determined to increase employee involvement in other areas. In addition, Murray & Roberts pioneered the Sunflower Projects, a training programme which began as a mix of the profit motive with community investment in training and job creation. Murray and Roberts is thus a useful case study to see how a traditional CSI programme may become more participatory and community-oriented.

Part of the interest in examining CSI at Murray & Roberts is the role Ractliffe's personality plays in giving it a distinctive stamp. For despite its seemingly autocratic approach, the company puts great emphasis on employee communication and the devolution of operations. Ractliffe is a communicator *par excellence* who loves his work and lets enthusiasms show when describing projects that he believes in. At the same time, he is aware that he alone cannot *be* the group's CSI. 'The company is a big believer in decentralisation, which puts responsibility as close to coalface as possible,' he explains. 'So you empower people, and don't have as much power yourself. Our job is to act as facilitator.'

What is not clear is the extent to which communication at Murray & Roberts is a two-way process. For while the company won a prize in 1994 for publishing one of South Africa's best employee reports, the report targets sophisticated readers and is inaccessible to employees who lack excellent English skills. (The group had over 47 000 employees in 1993.) The report contains summaries by chief executives at Murray & Roberts' business units that discuss employee education and training programmes, economic conditions, new developments and affirmative action. It also describes the group's key core values.

Ractliffe admits that the company has not advanced to the stage of others profiled here to support a quasi-developmental CSI programme or devolve it to the workforce. 'I don't think we've involved employees enough at the group level. We're not where Premier is; it's still a corporate-directed activity. But there's more discussion about how to coordinate the Foundation's activities with our operating groups and programmes,' he says.

Dialogues between management and employees by division or operating group are encouraged. Once Ractliffe spent three hours making a presentation to 120 cleaners and security guards in one operating group and found the feedback "very illuminating". And, according to Ractliffe, employee suggestions are welcome, although no formal structures for their involvement currently exist.

Still, Ractliffe is dedicated to driving the group toward change. After reading an article following the events of February 1990 that said that 'Business must still have its February 2', Ractliffe initiated workshops for executives and the general workforce with some of South Africa's top "change" consultants to address workplace concerns.

But in an affirmative action workshop in early 1994 to 85 top managers throughout the group, not one person was black and only one was a woman. The group takes a hard line against tokenism in affirmative action, and says it seeks to avoid destroying talented people through 'premature or over-promotion' or to 'chase away talented whites by creating the impression of a "closed shop" in favour of others'.

Having a presence

In common with his CSI counterparts elsewhere, Ractliffe takes a hands-on role with organisations to which Murray & Roberts contributes. He is a trustee of the JET and the DG Murray Trust, one of South Africa's biggest private charitable funders, whose education and finance committee he chairs. (The Trust was formed by Douglas Murray, one of Murray & Roberts' founders. Once the controlling shareholder of Murray & Roberts Holdings, the Trust is now completely independent of the group.)

In addition to summarising its CSI spending (which was budgeted at R6,6 million for 1995), Murray & Roberts' annual report features information on social policies regarding investment in employee training, housing and benefits, and community involvement. Budgeting 5 percent of the previous year's ordinary dividend to shareholders for social spending is a form of 'tithing', according to Ractliffe. 'I've since had other companies approach me about this,' he continues. 'It makes sense. You make profits; you keep some to reinvest; you give some to shareholders; and you give some to the communities in which you operate.'

A near-crisis turns into a win-win situation

Murray & Roberts' support of Sunflower Projects, which is some-times presented as CSI, was in fact not a social investment endeav-our, but designed as a for-profit spinoff to provide training in basic construction skills, plus literacy and numeracy to help participants become more marketable. Launched in 1985 and based in Durban, it aimed to channel profits into the Murray & Roberts Foundation for further social investment. Counting on an ongoing tie-in with the National Manpower Department, Sunflower marketed its ser-vices nationwide and built creches, schools, clinics and training centres. Some 60 000 people benefited from Sunflower training programmes.

The dependency on one client — Manpower — and one funder — Murray & Roberts — proved almost fatal. When the department reduced its support, Sunflower could no longer carry its full-time staff of 50 people and nearly closed down. In 1993, in order to carry on, Sunflower retrenched half its staff and became a not-for-gain company to raise funds elsewhere. It also changed its focus from exclusively training unskilled workers to upgrading the skills of black contractors in the communities in which it gets commissions. Murray & Roberts still provides some backing but wants Sunflower to become self-sufficient. Says Ractliffe bluntly: 'It's not cheque-book CSI.'

A focus on achievers

Certain key themes permeate Murray & Roberts' CSI. All funded projects must include community participation and involvement; be linked to a work and learning ethic; promote self-reliance, and lead to lasting improvements in the lives of participants.

In addition, it aims to support "key achievers" (such as its fund-ing of Africa's first chair in environmental education at Rhodes University, the annual Des Baker Award for Architecture and the chair in construction management at University of Cape Town) and promote cross-cultural relationship-building, such as programmes to "normalise" sports (the company built a cricket pitch in Alexandra township) and cultural activities. Among the latter, Murray & Roberts supports the annual Male Voice Choir Festival in Johannesburg, which joins black and white choirs.

The thrust of the company's CSI programme has changed from mostly donations towards specific project support, emphasising those that build skills the company will need. These include a bridg-ing programme at the Port Elizabeth Technikon, building management programmes at University of Cape Town, and computer training centres.

Most funding is concentrated in areas where Murray & Roberts has operations or employees live, and Ractliffe anticipates that Murray & Roberts' CSI will increasingly focus on projects which include its own people. This could lead to a format modelled on Premier's SICs, which encourage employee involvement at the grassroots level.

As part of its CSI, Murray & Roberts supported the construction of a learning centre in Tembisa, near corporate headquarters, which includes a primary school, adult literacy programme and a media centre. With funding from the Independent Development Trust, workers trained by Sunflower built the school, whose design included some playing fields, and Murray & Roberts agreed to contribute three VCRs if the community put in new grass on the fields. Ractliffe also particularly likes and has helped to fund Project ARK in Durban, a social services centre located in what used to be a "native" location for dockworkers.

Positive developments

Murray & Roberts was a major donor to JET and initiated the Positive Development News Initiative (PDNI), which aims to educate South Africans on positive projects nationwide, through print (including a newsletter) and television. *People,* a weekly NNTV series funded by PDNI, spotlights successful grassroots groups.

A favourite project of Ractliffe's, PDNI could come across as somewhat saccharine, since it represents a 'good news' media initiative rather than direct input to an organisation. Ractliffe insists otherwise. 'I'm in love with PDNI,' he says. 'It casts its net wide. It can help good projects be replicated elsewhere. It's an umbrella thing that's helping people to network. We desperately need disclosure of positive achievements to counter negative images.'

For example, a documentary exploring how poor rural women in the Transkei organised a self-help project can be a model for other communities. Furthermore, Ractliffe says, Marie Bruyns of Facet Films, the company producing *People,* provides apprenticeship opportunities for young blacks. PDNI is supported by a number of other companies, including Anglo American, Eskom, Nampak and Nedcor. Other funding comes from the DG Murray Trust, the Independent Development Trust and the Kagiso Trust.

Nedcor Community Development Fund
PO Box 1144
Johannesburg 2000
Phone: (011) 630-2207
Fax: (011) 630-2165

Summary:

The Nedcor Chairman's Fund was renamed the Nedcor Community Development Fund in late 1993 to reflect a changing emphasis from its origins and in its goals. It signalled a departure from traditional practices in which giving emanated from top executives' offices to a more participative grantmaking programme which, it so happens, is mostly run by women, and is becoming racially mixed as well. This effort can be attributed both to efforts by Fund director Hilary Ashton and her team to broaden its base and a general trend by more enlightened companies to make sure that CSI is more connected to the communities in which they operate. But Nedcor's Community Development Fund has gone much further, doing hands-on development work (often using "human power" rather than money), and branching into areas where the Nedcor Group does not have obvious direct involvement, such as in rural areas.

*   *   *

The Nedcor Chairman's Fund was renamed the Nedcor Community Development Fund late in 1993 to reflect its evolution from a donations programme emanating from the chairman's office to an education trust and, finally, a proactive development programme. Under the leadership of Senior Manager Hilary Ashton, the Fund is making its mark supporting grassroots projects throughout much of South Africa, with a growing emphasis on rural areas.

Until the early 1980s, according to Ashton, Nedcor exercised what she calls the 'very worst' form of CSI, signing cheques and sending them to universities. Then, toward the end of the decade, Nedcor joined Old Mutual in commissioning a social, political and economic "scenario planning" exercise to examine how the two companies could remain profitable, relevant and meaningful as South Africa surged toward what everyone then realised would be an inevitable transition to majority rule. The completed study called on the private sector to increase substantially its investment in education, housing and job creation if the transition were to succeed — in other words, the RDP.

For a huge financial organisation like Nedcor, the new emphasis, including support for projects in areas where mainstream banks are unheard-of, might seem out-of-place. But it is part of the Nedcor Group's long-term strategy, explains Ashton, a former English teacher who joined Nedcor's training department in 1989 and took over the Fund in 1992. 'We see CSI as a facilitation process that will affect society and economic empowerment for people previously precluded from enjoying access to equal opportunity,' she says.

To finance this process, the group allocates 1,3 percent of after-tax profits to the Fund, which constitutes about half of Nedcor's total CSI programming. The balance goes through so-called "mutually beneficial marketing" — a euphemism for "cause-related marketing" programmes such as the Green Trust and various arts and sports sponsorships that carry the Nedbank name. These programmes are coordinated by Ivan May, Assistant General Manager, Nedcor Bank Marketing Services. It is probably tempting for the company to direct more of its CSI monies toward marketing if it boosts Nedbank's visibility, and Ashton is fiercely determined to keep the Fund autonomous.

Following the presentation of the scenarios, Nedcor committed itself to spending up to R55 million on entrepreneurial development, education and human resources development for the following five years. Each affiliate company would contribute a percentage of profits. Ashton had expected R5,5 million for 1994, but since 1993 was a profitable year for the group, she had access to R8 million instead.

An interesting aspect of the Nedcor Community Development's Fund structure is the extent to which it is deliberately women-led. One of Ashton's team's driving reasons to rename the Chairman's Fund was because of the white male "old South Africa" that the previous name implied. Nowadays four of the Fund's five staff members are female; the exception is a young black man named Alex Monyai, a former public relations student who serves as a database clerk and public relations assistant. Ashton plans to train him to become a field worker and project evaluator.

The other three staff include a general office administrator who also handles some public relations; a financial controller who monitors all donations and spending; and a professional development worker, Nanette Cooper, who helps projects in the Northern and Western Transvaal, the Free State and a portion of the Northern Cape, and shares project work in Gauteng with Ashton. Ashton, who spends about 80 percent of her time visiting projects, focuses on KwaZulu/Natal and on the Northern, Western and Eastern Cape.

The department currently falls under Nedcor's public affairs division, which in November 1994 was incorporated into the new RDP and Corporate Affairs Division headed by Divisional Director Lot Ndlovu, former executive director of the Black Management Forum.

Ashton is the only woman on the Fund's management committee, whose representatives come from each of Nedcor's contributing companies. She is pushing the trustees to democratise the committee and to include employees. In addition, since she sees CSI to be substantially an affirmative action programme, Ashton believes that she and other white staff will 'have to work ourselves out of a job. I don't see myself here in another three years,' she says.

Increasing transparency

Communicating what it does is a strong component of the Nedcor Fund's activities. An outside public relations consultant once handled the Nedcor Fund account, but it now arranges its own events to promote its role in projects. Internally, the Fund is becoming much more transparent: at the end of the 1994 fiscal year, the company was preparing a Nedcor Community Development Fund report which would list spending by category, such as educare, secondary education and the percentage spent on administration, plus the contributions to the Fund by each Nedcor member company.

The Nedcor Fund's largest grants, worth more than R300 000 each, include the Joint Enrichment Programme, a youth development initiative; The Valley Trust and Project Literacy (see the Profiles on p167, p190, and p174).

Facilitation rather than funds

The Fund has developed a grants application form and its evaluation process can take a while. 'We fund nothing we can't see,' states Ashton. 'Our dialogues with organisations can take up to nine months' — a marked contrast to the rapid response style of the Anglo American and De Beers Chairman's Fund. But sometimes money is 'an afterthought', she says, since the Fund's role also includes involvement and facilitation.

'When we're convinced a project has merit, we give the community or group an application form. We review all proposals we get, but the form makes the process more efficient.' Ashton believes that the form also helps groups do a better job thinking through how they will use a grant. When necessary — if, for instance, there are language problems — Ashton and her staff help the groups fill out the form, so no one is excluded from applying.

Like the Liberty Life Foundation, the Nedcor Community Development Fund's activities have grown quickly in a short time — but not its staff. As a result, says Ashton, 'We fell into the same bottleneck experienced problem by some NGOs: we realised we wouldn't have enough money to service new projects. We generally undertake to support projects for three years and must ensure that some organisations don't become too dependent on us, so we need to alert them to seek other sources of support.'

In September 1993, it looked as though the Fund might not be able to take on new projects, and Ashton and her staff took time out to ponder their next steps. They mapped out a five-year budget plan. 'It was a frightening process — and an important learning experience,' she explains. 'No projects suffered but we put new projects on hold until July 1994.'

Proactive partnerships

Nedcor is increasingly working in partnership with other funders. 'Compacts are the wave of the future,' feels Ashton. For instance, its support for Project Literacy's pilot programme at a minimum-security prison was co-funded with Liberty Life and JCI, among others. (Nedcor sponsored a programme visit and reception to announce its donations, while none of the other principal funders, some of whom gave more, did the same; it is not their style.)

A more deliberate partnership resulted in a successful water provision project in Mafefe, a poor, drought-stricken region in Lebowa comprising some 30 villages. The community took most of the initiative, Ashton says, drawing on outside technical and financial assistance. Residents formed a water committee to organise a way to get clean water for bathing, drinking and farming. A number of NGOs, including Operation Hunger and the Rural Advice Centre (RAC), were already operating there; Nedcor had donated R100 000 to RAC, of which R20 000 went to the project. (RAC was liquidated in 1993, following serious management problems.)

Spring water was available, but because tapping straight into it would have meant, to the community, that this was interfering with the ancestors, they had to find new ways to tap and purify it. First the committee identified a water source, and then, with technical help, built tanks and improvised a type of British ram pump to bring the water into the villages, which are in rocky, dry areas. Committee members did all the digging and organising and raised the funds to pay for it.

'They are very strong people who won't be ridden over by anyone,' says Ashton. A partnership with Toyota resulted in finding a dealer in Pietersburg who understood what type of vehicle the community needed, and Toyota provided it at cost. Toyota also helped with vehicle registration, licensing and sign writing.

Nedcor has recently shifted much of its energy toward rural projects. The Fund was the principal funder of a Participatory Rural Appraisal conference in 1993, which brought together leaders from 50 rural NGOs. An important initiative, the conference cost just R4 000 to sponsor. Nedcor is particularly interested in supporting of The Valley Trust's efforts to 'export' its projects beyond its base in rural Natal. Since late 1993, the Fund has collaborated with the Trust, community leaders in Vosloorus, and Air Caterers, a company that provides airline food, on a pilot feeding scheme in the East Rand township.

Now known as the Valley Trust Nutrition Education Project, it arose when a Nedcor manager approached Ashton, observing that 'tons' of uneaten airline food were being thrown away every week and wondering if there weren't a way to obtain it for a feeding programme. Ashton approached Air Caterers and arranged to retrieve its packaged foods. (Fresh food, even if untouched, may not be legally reused.) The community group, joined by The Valley Trust's nutrition experts, devised a distribution programme to feed people in township schools and squatter camps.

The project created jobs for seven people to take food from conveyor belts, and, in a contracted taxi, to pick it up. The programme, which now also includes a food gardens project, feeds 6 000 people. Mondi Paper is sponsoring an income-generating recycling programme there, and dairy company Clover will assist similar feeding schemes to be run at six or seven pilot schools in the Eastern Free State and the Western Transvaal.

Bringing back her "South Africanness"
Running a CSI programme, Ashton has found, is physically and emotionally exhausting — and exhilarating. Drawing on models of accountability, stewardship and teamwork which she has studied in the writings of US development expert David Korten, Ashton has learned to draw energy from her work, and she loves it. 'It has returned my South Africanness to me, restored parts of my South

African identity which were robbed by apartheid,' she says.

One particularly transforming moment came when Edgar Luthuli, son of ANC leader Albert Luthuli, took her on a visit of his father's village of Groutville, in northern Natal, introduced her to Luthuli's widow and showed her his father's church and grave. 'His life until then had seemed like a shadow, but the grave reminded me that he had been a father and a husband.' Nearby, the new Albert Luthuli Community and Educational Development Centre offers job and entrepreneurship training and educational skills, and includes a community centre with a theatre and meeting rooms, supported by Nedcor and other funders.

Elsewhere, Ashton has been moved by what she calls the 'spirit-opening experience' of seeing people's competence and skills in poor, isolated communities. In particular, she cites the efforts by poor women who crush rocks into gravel and sell it, and also attend adult literacy classes together. 'Everywhere else rock-crushing is a symbol of bondage but it was liberating these women,' suggests Ashton. Nedcor gave the women R5 000 and wheelbarrows.

Optimism about the role companies can play
Despite the demands of her job, Ashton is exhilarated by her work and optimistic about the role companies can play. 'The development abyss is so deep that the state will never be able to take control of it all,' she declares. And while the development community and corporate establishment find themselves at loggerheads in other countries, in South Africa, she believes, they can learn to work together in a positive way. 'I don't think there's a team of corporates as devoted as South African corporates,' she says.

Pick 'n Pay
PO Box 23087
Claremont 7735
Phone: (021) 658-1000
Fax: (021) 683-2514

Summary:

Marketing and CSI are one at Pick 'n Pay, which has developed some of the most sophisticated and transparent social programmes among South African corporates. In addition, its CSI is defined in a holistic manner to include internal employee issues. Pick 'n Pay publishes a full social report, separate from its annual report, which not only lists all social investment spending (although not itemised to individual grantees, which is difficult given the decentralised nature of the company), but also describes its employee training initiatives and benefits, including parental leave, retirement, share and incentive schemes.

*   *   *

There's not even a thin line to distinguish marketing at Pick 'n Pay from its CSI. CSI, according to the company's Marketing Director Martin Rosen, whose department operates it, *is* marketing, and he has no problem linking the two, despite his awareness of occasional bad-mouthing by other large companies, within CSI circles, for doing so. 'Is CSI marketing? Is it boosting our brand at the *expense* of employees? Is it advertising?' he asks rhetorically. It's all part of the same thing. If you make a donation as a retailer, you also build brand and bring in customers. So, according to Pick 'n Pay, CSI "adds value" to the company — a term that permeates its annual and social reports.

In the process, Pick 'n Pay, which prefers to calls its programmes corporate responsibility, has attracted attention for its support of events such as the annual Argus Pick 'n Pay cycle tour in Cape Town, which raises money for the Rotary Club; its efforts to bring the 2004 Olympics to Cape Town; and its sponsorship of "green" products along with recycling facilities and environmental information centres that promote environmental awareness — and the Pick 'n Pay brand.

No other supermarket chain has engaged the public so directly nor developed such a strong identity as a "green" company. Yes, it combines marketing with CSI, as Rosen sees it, and in the shrewdest possible way.

This strategy coincides with Pick 'n Pay's independence. A family-controlled company founded in 1968, its founder-chairman, Raymond Ackerman, spends considerable time overseas studying state-of-the-art models in the retail industry rather than maintaining an inward view of how South African business should operate. (Rosen does the same.) In addition, there are fewer layers of bureaucracy to go through in order to implement new programmes.

As a result, Pick 'n Pay has adopted some marketing and operational approaches, such as the early introduction of laser-scanners at its checkout points and recycling facilities for customers who bring in bottles, plastics, tins and paper, that are more in line with US or British models than with local counterparts. Moreover, to repeat Rosen, it's brilliant marketing. Customers who want to recycle household disposables can combine recycling with shopping. The proceeds from recycling are used to fund environmental projects.

Sophisticated social disclosure
Pick 'n Pay is ahead of the pack in social disclosure. It produces separate social and environmental reports that contain far more detail than most South African companies are currently prepared to disclose — but which would look at home among a pile of US corporate social reports. (As with many of its US counterparts, Pick 'n Pay prints the reports on recycled paper and notes this on the back covers.)

Its 1994 annual report devotes nine pages to the company's environmental activities, including a discussion of its 1989 announcement, promoted through the national media, of a company-wide environmental initiative. Pick 'n Pay claims to be the first South African firm to be so proactive; its programme includes a pledge to address 14 environmental issues within company operations and communities. Many of these are tied to market activities, and link the Pick 'n Pay name with environmental involvement. (A photograph of teenagers engaged in a river clean-up shows them wearing Pick 'n Pay plastic aprons, and its Superstores launched a "Save our Planet" campaign, with cash prizes.)

In 1993, Pick 'n Pay hired a specialist to conduct an environmental audit and make recommendations for further action. These include sponsoring community activities in waste collection and sorting, which can double as job-creation projects tied to the RDP, "adopting" schools with an environmental focus, and expanding in-house environmental policies.

While many local firms limit social reporting to their external CSI, Pick 'n Pay's social report features a section on internal employee programmes, including a discussion of its affirmative action philosophy and the programmes it runs to promote it (training, communication and employee benefits in housing, parental leave, medical aid, share schemes, and so on). (Pick 'n Pay reported 27 000 employees in 1994.)

Affirmative action has not, however, hit the higher echelons of management, as a review of the company's annual report reveals; nor are any blacks on the board of directors. Hiring is merit-based only, says Rosen, who notes that more blacks are reaching the shop management level. However, Pick 'n Pay is using market targets to create a new layer of black managers: it is embarking on a programme to offer franchises to blacks to run Pick 'n Pay stores in townships. This is still new and had not yet made much impact, however, but negotiations with black businessmen are ongoing.

The social report describes major funding categories, some projects that were funded, and, in many cases, the amount of money donated to them. At the end is a list of all organisations to which Pick 'n Pay contributed in 1993/4, including a total rand value (R6,4 million) and a breakdown of giving by five categories: community development and housing (R3,2 million, or 49 percent); sports development (R1,7 million, 27 percent); education (R1,3 million, 21 percent); environment (R150 000, 2 percent), and arts and culture (R73 000, 1 percent).

The company claims to donate between 6 and 8 percent of post-tax profits toward community upliftment. This amount excludes the company's investment in employee training programmes, which is about R4,4 million annually. 'The more transparent you become the more support you get,' says Rosen. Pick 'n Pay won the overall prize in *The Weekly Mail*'s 1992 "Investing in the Future" competition, with special honours for its environmental initiatives.

In addition to containing general descriptions of CSI, the report describes some major funded programmes in detail, along with the amount donated to them. Examples of larger grants was R200 000 to the 1993 Comrades Marathon; a R200 000 pledge to the 1994 *Sowetan* nation-building project to support parenting workshops; and a four-year R100 000 pledge to the Women's Bureau of South Africa. Most grants range from R10 000 to R50 000. And Pick 'n Pay often runs programmes as part of a community matching initiative. For example, Pick 'n Pay helped raise funds through a special Golf Day to sponsor disabled athletes at the 1993 Special Olympics World Games and ran an in-store campaign for customer donations to the Hospice Association of South Africa.

Top-down management style

Despite its transparency, Pick 'n Pay appears to run its CSI in an autocratic manner emanating from Rosen's office at Pick 'n Pay Bedfordview branch and from head offices in Cape Town. The core marketing staff consists of him, four 'communications' experts and a secretary. Employees do not have input in offering ideas or making giving decisions, although that is changing, but on a small scale. Anne Sayers, National Consumer Affairs Manager, monitors regional community programmes, including 'brag books' that list local projects. But the compiling of such books appears to be *ad hoc*, and each regional manager may decide whether or not to encourage employee involvement.

When it works, it can work well. The company sponsors "green groups" of employees who take part in projects such as community clean-ups and tree planting, and it circulates an in-house *Environment Update* informing employees of companywide "green" projects.

In a move to enhance the image of local stores in their communities, Rosen often arranges for a cheque to an organisation to be handed over by a store manager in its region. 'One of the biggest things we've learned is that the cheque should come from store managers so that the managers know about money that's being spent,' Rosen remarks. 'We used just to mail the cheque from headquarters. I think we do more hands-on that way than anyone.' However, the 'hands-on' seems to apply to who actually holds the cheque. Little follow-up monitoring on donations takes place — a problem that Rosen acknowledges is one of his department's weaknesses.

Perhaps for that reason, Rosen calls Ithuba Trust, a programme that raises and distributes funds for social causes that promote self-reliance, one of the projects he likes best. 'It's a good way to raise money, and it gets millions of rand to good groups in a short time,' he says. Rosen takes sharp exception to critics of Ithuba who claim that the organisation keeps a lot of the funds raised for administration. 'Do an investigation yourself,' he replies, recommending a visit to its offices.

No CSI with unions

Unions have no input in Pick 'n Pay's CSI. And despite the company's careful shaping of its image as a kinder, gentler place to shop, it has a mixed reputation for service and was the target of one of South Africa's first major post-election strikes. Staged by the South African Commercial, Catering and Allied Workers Union (SACCAWU), it included workers rampaging through some stores in defiance of an agreement with the company. (The origins of the strike are muddy regarding the new leadership of SACCAWU, and the dispute was settled following mediation in which the union came out with a pay package little different from Pick 'n Pay's original offer.)

Rosen concedes that company has received 'chronic complaints about customer service', which he attributes to disputes over union recognition. 'The easiest way to vent frustration as an employee is to take it out on your customers,' he notes. Rosen indicated that the company will now become "firmer and less tolerant" and would not compromise on discipline.

During the strike, the union criticised Pick 'n Pay for spending money on projects it considered irrelevant to community and national needs, such as its 'hospitality' packages to promote the South African Olympic team for the 1996 Olympic Games in Atlanta, Georgia. Rosen counters that its support, using the 'Olympic hopeful' theme, develops local athletes. And for one year, 1 percent of the profits from sales of the company's house brand will go to Olympic training. 'Everyone benefits,' claims Rosen, since the company negotiated better prices from suppliers for the promotion, enabling it to pass on a price savings to consumers.

And although Rosen acknowledges the need for more employee input in CSI, he explicitly excludes unions from this process. 'That's not where the action is,' he states.

Even so, Pick 'n Pay's family-related benefits, particularly its generous parental leave for new mothers *and* fathers, rank among the best in its sector. In a survey of "caring" companies, Pick 'n Pay ranked number one among whites and number four among blacks. The company also sponsors a parenting programme in conjunction with the *Sowetan* newspaper, which first approached Pick 'n Pay about the project.

The Premier Group Social Investment Councils
PO Box 1530
Johannesburg 2000
Phone: (011) 446-2231
Fax: (011) 446-2239

Summary:

The Premier Group's Social Investment Councils (SICs), in which management and employees share decision-making powers, represent a bold and difficult initiative in South Africa. A national council, a national projects committee plus seven regional councils make decisions on community funding projects. This is not an easy undertaking; managing the councils is a labour-intensive effort and one person is charged with overseeing their operation nationwide. But they can foster a healthy synergy between management and workers, and address trade union criticisms that workers don't have enough input in CSI policy-making by devolving CSI responsibility on them.

*   *   *

The dominant theme of CSI at Premier is getting management and employees working together. (For this reason, a union member who has been very involved was also interviewed.) This has been achieved — with great effort, and not always smoothly — through the creation of Social Investment Councils (SICs), unique among South African companies. These include seven regional SICs, a National Council and a National Projects Committee (NPC). Membership on all consists of equal numbers of elected employees (mainly trade union members) and managers appointed by Premier's Human Resources Department; chairmanship of the councils rotates annually between management and worker members.

About 60 to 80 employees are involved at a given time; some regional council members also serve on the National Council. They identify worthy community projects, choose which will get funds and monitor them. Administrator Diana McGurk oversees the process; she reports to Corrie Cloete, Premier's Human Resources Director. Her job is highly time-intensive, and requires her to attend most SIC regional meetings. Her only direct support comes from a shared secretary.

It is important to note that the SICs focus on regional CSI giving, which claims 62 percent of Premier's CSI budget. The balance goes to tertiary and technikon education. Spending decisions in this area are taken by the NPC, which is made up of three management and three worker representatives. Premier's one sports promotion is funded by the company's marketing department and the proceeds given to charity. The Human Resources Department oversees a bursary programme to cover studies in work-related disciplines and is funded separately.

The regional SIC funding priorities cover three main areas: 1) education programmes *not* funded by the NPC, primarily "train the trainer" projects, adult basic education and pre-school educare, which get 45 percent of the total; 2) self-help and welfare projects, which together get another 45 percent of funds; and 3) conservation and culture, which get the remaining 10 percent. The company also has an "emergency discretionary fund" for urgent purposes, such as helping the Red Cross to distribute blankets to farm workers in the Eastern Transvaal during a brutally cold winter. Premier allocates 1,5 percent of after-tax revenues for CSI, not including bursaries.

Origins

The SICs came about after management, with the endorsement of then-CE Peter Wrighton, devised an alternative to the traditional top-down approach to CSI that they felt addressed worker concerns about their lack of involvement. (Wrighton announced his retirement from the Premier Group in 1994.) By involving workers and mid-level managers, this approach would, they felt, yield better results.

The reality has been mixed. Managing the SICs has turned out to be a complex process. On one hand, says Sebei Motsoeneng, a shop steward with the Food and Allied Workers Union (Fawu, Premier's biggest union), the SICs have 'empowered us more than we ever expected'. At the time of the Premier interview, Motsoeneng sat on both the national SIC and the Wits/Vaal regional SIC. But the track record of union and management involvement has been erratic in terms of attending meetings and project follow-through.

Starting the councils in the first place was difficult. It took 18 months for trade unions to agree to take part, and until then no workers volunteered to join because of their wariness about working with management. Then the company approached union leaders, who agreed to sit on the council — but skipped the meetings. Corrie Cloete, who had already involved unions in running their pension and provident funds, medical aid schemes and housing and bursary programmes, spurred a turnaround: he negotiated with the unions to join the SICs, and this time they agreed.

Once that barrier was broken, says Motsoeneng, 'There was no real resistance. I've been involved almost since the beginning. We deal with matters as a committee rather than as union and management.' But conflicts remain in areas such as wage negotiations and conditions of employment.

However, the union committee members (all shop stewards) faced a further barrier to full participation: financial illiteracy — a lack of understanding of how budgets are drawn up, how programmes are funded, and, more fundamentally, how to interpret corporate financial statements. Premier responded by compiling a course on basic financial understanding which examines how to interpret group financial figures and other data. Designed initially for shop stewards, the course is now offered companywide as part of its literacy initiative.

For Motsoeneng the financial programme was an eye-opener: 'I'd never been exposed to this area at all. I've learned a lot.' With more worker participation, programme administration is less paternalistic. 'The ultimate success of the SICs depends on the ability to empower workers through literacy to participate and understand how business works.'

Mixing head office and regional concerns

Project screening begins at head office, usually drawing on outside appeals sent to the company. If the project falls within established criteria, it is referred to the appropriate regional council. These could cover such community projects as creches, special school programmes, educare, technical skills, teacher upgrading and basic adult skills. A hefty 80 to 90 percent of these get some funding. Large projects may be funded for three years while others are 'one-offs'. Projects of urgent social concern, such as feeding schemes, will not be terminated if the need remains.

Despite the devolution of decision-making, Premier's CSI budget is centralised at corporate headquarters in Johannesburg, where all cheques are signed. (Some companies prefer to decentralise their budgets as a way to encourage local input.) Strict accountability is important. 'We had one mistake but not a big one,' recalls McGurk. 'An employee told us about a dance school and we gave R3 000 for training, but the money was used to buy cameras.' Fortunately, this is the exception rather than the rule.

Premier used to support huge institutions, but now focuses more on grassroots community service groups. The company has drastically cut its donations to some large NGOs in the process, says McGurk, in part because the unions opposed funding them.

What other companies can learn

Despite their successes, the SICs have had problems that other firms should know of if they may want to form their own. The logistics can be nightmarish; regional meetings sometimes do not reach a quorum, and McGurk, who attends as many as she can, sometimes travels a long distance to attend a meeting that has been cancelled.

Also, McGurk has found that union SIC members sometimes recommend funding organisations that are not well-enough established to get the type of funding Premier wants to give. To that end, she tries to steer the SICs towards groups that have a track record. Still, the SICs are willing to consider new, non-registered groups for grants as long as they can fill in a standardised questionnaire and can show that they have the resources to do what they say. From management's side, there have been problems of SIC members who are not fully committed. 'They need to be people-oriented,' says McGurk. Most SIC management delegates are human resources personnel.

Among the Premier-funded projects McGurk admires most are The Valley Trust, a socio-economic development programme near Durban, and LIMA, a rural development project on Natal's South Coast. (See the profiles on p190 and p171.) The Valley Trust is considered a model of integrated programming, transparency and solid financial management. Among its many projects, LIMA empowers small farmers to rent agricultural land and equipment and market their produce and has involved women in building roads and dams and planting trees. McGurk admits to having been sceptical about LIMA, but then visited and found that coordinator Duncan Stewart had 'moved mountains'. Premier's grant to LIMA is modest: in 1992-3, it was just R10 000, and the year before it was R4 000.

Indeed, most grants are modest. With the exception of projects such as a two-year pledge of R350 000 to the crisis centre at Baragwanath Hospital in 1990-1 and a two-year donation of R100 000 to the Wits Technikon Business Development Programme, grants rarely exceed R25 000; they generally range between R10 000 to R15 000. Among small grants generated by the SIC was R20 000 to a workshop for disabled people at the Orange Farm settlement recommended by an employee who chaired the Witwatersrand

Council, and a grant to Work for Africa, an organisation that helps develop small businesses.

Can the model be transferred?

Can other companies follow Premier's suit? Some have contacted Premier for advice, but none (except perhaps AECI) has tried this model. An important factor before launching SICs is to make sure that the company's own house is in order first. Keeping communication channels open is key. 'We have a holistic approach in lots of our joint committees between management and unions,' says Corrie Cloete. 'The shop stewards on the National Council are used to interaction, so it's more of a problem-solving than a conflict approach. If another company wants to form SICs and hasn't had the tradition of close management/union interaction, it won't get cooperation.'

Glossy brochures are not part of Premier's approach; neither is full disclosure. CSI is summarised in Premier's annual report, projects are discussed in its in-house newsletter, and unions report back to members on SICs. But Premier does not publish data on CSI spending.

Despite the drawbacks, Premier deserves credit for taking its pioneering action. 'Our philosophy is that actions speak louder than words,' maintains Cloete. 'Other companies might say what they're *going* to do. We can say what we're doing now.'

Changes

Premier has joined the trend to cooperate on projects with other firms. 'We realise that we can be a far greater force by working together. It's great for me to be able to pick up the phone and speak to a colleague about a project,' says McGurk, who was personal assistant to Tony Bloom, Peter Wrighton's predecessor, before she took her current job. 'Companies used to be afraid they'd lose their identity if they get into a "pot", but it's different now; we can keep our identities. Companies are not using CSI so much as a marketing tool, and everyone is very helpful.'

But McGurk remains concerned about the cultural divides she experiences when visiting projects. 'I feel conscious when I speak with a black person and talk about things I've been doing because of the privileges I have that they can't do. After politics and the job, what now?' This discomfort has made her feel more than ever that SICs play an important role in responding to genuine community needs.

In short, the partnership theme within the SICs as well as among CSI professionals reflects an overall trend toward cooperation, which McGurk hopes will develop between government, NGOs and the funding community. 'I hope corporate donors and government will work together to good result,' she concludes.

Shell South Africa
PO Box 2231
Cape Town 8000
Phone: (021) 408-4911
Fax: (021) 25-3807

Summary:

Shell was known for a proactive, highly visible CSI programme for much of the decade prior to Nelson Mandela's release from prison and the legalisation of the ANC and other political organisations. This included extensive financial support for the alternative press which served as the public conscience of the political opposition. Shell's current strategy is to implement its CSI programme to meet guidelines of the RDP. By placing people like Maurice Radebe (Transvaal CSI manager), a former student activist with a background in science, business and grassroots work, into the CSI "hot seats", the company has shown an awareness of the role CSI can play in South Africa's road to redevelopment with good connections to the new government.

*   *   *

Shell South Africa — a subsidiary of Royal Dutch Shell, one of the world's largest corporations — found itself in a sometimes unwanted limelight during the sanctions era as the target of an international boycott by anti-apartheid campaigners who protested the company's ongoing involvement in South Africa. The oil giant had no intention of disinvesting and took the strategic decision that as long as it was operating in South Africa it would take a proactive, public stance against government apartheid policies even though the government remained a key client.

Originally running its CSI according to conventional public relations models, Shell switched gears in the early 1980s to become one of the first companies to come out publicly against apartheid. Its new strategy, which included significant and visible support for human rights and the independent press, was spearheaded by Coleen Bracher, a veteran of student politics who was then Shell's general manager for public affairs. While Maurice Radebe concedes that the policy probably arose in partial response to international pressure, it also represented a commitment rare among companies in South Africa.

Bracher would not have been able to implement the programme without support from Shell's top management. Shell has been long involved in heavy-duty scenario planning and could see that a democratic order was coming, so it made business sense to head in that direction. Readers of *The Weekly Mail* and other then-struggling "alternative" publications became used to seeing full-page advertisements from Shell advocating democracy and an unfettered press. These contributions helped keep the publications alive.

In the new era, Shell's CSI has changed gears significantly, as it no longer needs to turn its attention to groups protesting the government. Placed within the company's public affairs department, headed by General Manager of Public Affairs Humphrey Khoza, one of the nation's highest-ranked black business executives, Shell's CSI, as at many other major SA corporations, is forging partnerships with government and civic organisations as funder and project facilitator.

This strategy is linked with the RDP, with emphases on job creation and education. The programme itself is coordinated by three regional managers: Radebe in Gauteng; Simone Le Hane, who covers the Cape Province; and Durban-based Lora Rossler, whose region includes KwaZulu/Natal and the Free State. Each one moved into public affairs after several years in other departments, where they learned the ropes of the business. They have field workers and other support staff to assist their CSI programmes. Radebe was the only one of these managers to be interviewed, as was Humphrey Khoza.

The company's CSI operates on a R15 million annual budget but Radebe did not say how this amount is set. From about 1989 through 1994, it invested over R50 million on education projects. The regional public affairs managers may approve projects up to R30 000. Higher sums go through Humphrey Khoza's office.

As a wholly-owned unit of an overseas firm, Shell South Africa is not obliged to publish a comprehensive annual financial report. However, it does produce a Business Report which summarises the performance of its exploration, manufacturing and retail operations as well as its environmental and social performance. The last item covers human resources concerns as well as CSI. The CSI budget includes six areas, allocated as follows: education (64 percent of the budget); job and wealth creation (12 percent); human rights (8 percent); environment (10 percent); arts and culture (3 percent), and health education (3 percent). The "Shell Road to Fame" — a highly visible multi-media project which includes a popular television talent show — is funded from a separate budget.

The 1992 report — the most recent available at the time of our interview — lists all recipients of CSI funds, but not how much the company gave them. The eight richly illustrated pages devoted to CSI are anecdotal and focus on a handful of projects, mainly in educational media and human rights. This approach is useful in describing the operation and impact of certain projects, but gives little information on Shell's actual involvement.

Linking CSI to the bottom line

Shell is increasingly tying its CSI with business imperatives, a new direction for its public affairs programme. Previously, Shell's CSI managers served mainly as community liaisons, evaluating projects for donations and conducting a straightforward form of follow-up.

This combination of new business linkages with demands of the RDP have created a new context for Shell's CSI. 'It's not enough just to know the players among NGOs, in the development world and at universities,' Radebe points out. 'Now we have to look at the *implication* of grants on our business,' including debates on public policy and the role that business must play. So Shell is now networking with the national government as well as ministries and departments on the provincial and local levels.

Humphrey Khoza, a major player in this area, notes that by its nature and size, Shell has a social responsibility to benefit the country through commercial investment (including risk-taking, innovation and economic impact), research and development (including new technologies) and income generation. But the RDP itself promotes a much greater interface between social investment and business by its all-inclusive nature. 'We didn't used to engage with our retail or chemicals units,' observes Radebe.

A particularly sensitive area for Shell concerns the acquisition of land for service development. Before the April 1994 elections, the company dealt directly with the old government. Nowadays Shell must contend with new players, such as national, provincial and local authorities, some of which might prefer that land be used for housing or other people-driven development. To avert the potential for friction, Shell has entered into partnerships with organisations such as South African National Civic Organisation (Sanco) and facilitates and helps to fund training initiatives to forge community/business partnerships. Shell foresees a bigger role in supporting the growth of black-owned small and medium enterprises, a linchpin of the RDP.

Shell's employee involvement in CSI is limited and union members are not involved, in part because of a history of strained relationships with management. If they want to raise issues regarding CSI, they are referred to the industrial relations and human resources departments. Even so, employees who know about good projects can contact Radebe or his colleagues through informal channels as well as a formal "community grant scheme" which assists employees involved in good community projects or who serve on NGO boards. This programme tends to target upper management and had slowed down in recent years, although the company expects it may be revived as part of its RDP involvement.

The company also believes that the owners of Shell's 800 service stations can play a role in CSI. They employ thousands more workers, and if some CSI is devolved to dealers, says Radebe, they can develop better community relations and a high local profile.

Another road to fame

A major new initiative by Shell, still in development as this profile was being prepared, is a competition to highlight new entrepreneurial talent. Modelled on the "Shell Road to Fame", a national performing arts competition which brought stardom to gospel singer Rebecca Malope after she won it, "Shell Live Wire" will identify young self-starters with their own small businesses and give them exposure and support to help them expand.

'This programme creates a culture of self-employment as an option for young blacks,' explains Radebe. 'We've been a community of job-seekers rather than job creators. Our economy can't absorb all matriculants. This new emphasis helps give people control over their lives.' Shell, which is drawing on a successful British prototype which in over a decade has produced more than 50 000 young entrepreneurs, plans to have pilot programmes under way in the Gauteng province in early 1995 and then to launch the programme nationwide. If the series succeeds locally, it will yield multiple benefits, including excellent publicity for the Shell brand and possibly increased customer loyalty.

Shell also puts substantial funding into education, with a heavy emphasis on teacher upgrading in formal and non-formal settings. In 1985, it established the Shell Maths and Science Centre, a major upgrading effort for secondary school teachers in Natal. The programme was renamed the Centre for the Advancement of Science and Mathematics Education (CASME) when other funders, including the Independent Development Trust, stepped in to enable it to expand, although Shell remains the principal donor and has several executives on CASME's board. The company is also a significant donor to READ and through a separate budget from its CSI allocation supports the JET, on whose board Humphrey Khoza sits.

Monitoring projects: Pros and cons

Radebe makes an interesting point regarding project monitoring. In the 'old' South Africa, this was a difficult and sensitive task, particularly in the late 1980s, when for political reasons it was unwise to press groups working to challenge government policy to open their books. Such exposure could threaten their existence. 'People were underground and it was hard to get these groups to account,' he says. 'In the human rights category, we supported initiatives like the Legal Resources Centre when they challenged forced removals. Many community organisations had been banned and were opposition groups. Even adult education and advice centres were highly politicised.'

But the unbanning of formerly outlawed organisations has led to new dynamic between donors and grantees, and for Shell, as at other companies, financial accountability is very important. 'Now we require regular reports, and now some groups are not getting money they had expected,' he explains. 'It's key to make sure they're achieving their goals. For most we want something twice a year; on rare occasions we just require an annual report.' Like their counterparts at other firms, Shell's public affairs managers sometimes serve on the boards of organisations the company supports. Shell occasionally commissions independent evaluations of troubled projects, in an effort to help them redirect effort or cut losses.

How he got there

Maurice Radebe has taken a roundabout but strategic route into managing Shell's CSI programme. He received a degree in applied maths and physics from the University of the North and a higher education diploma from Wits University, with an emphasis on adult education. During his student days he realised that he preferred hands-on development work to research. 'While I was studying, I was also teaching literacy and helping students prepare for matric,' he says. 'When I finished my degree I knew I didn't want to be in a laboratory.' He has also graduated from a Management Advanced Programme (MAP) at the Wits Business School and is currently completing an MBA there.

From university he joined World Vision as a project co-ordinator. He ran six projects, including a feeding scheme. Intrinsic to each project was an element of self-help. Aid recipients had to put some management input into them. So, for instance, Radebe helped feeding scheme members open a bank account so that they could buy food and monitor spending. This approach doubled as an adult learning process and reduced the dependency syndrome endemic to many such projects. Similarly, the participants in sewing and knitting projects had to coordinate their output so that garments were not produced that could not be sold.

Shell South Africa recruited Radebe from World Vision to become a public affairs officer and help coordinate Shells' adult education and community development programmes. Radebe wanted a broader exposure to business, so he spent several years in its retailing division, helping to build service stations before he joined the public affairs department.

Understanding CSI's "customer base"

For the time being, Maurice Radebe believes that black people are in a better position to manage CSI programmes. 'Customers of CSI are disadvantaged people, and they stand a better chance of being understood when the CSI administrators come from similar backgrounds. Some whites can do the job very well if they transcend barriers of apartheid, but historically it makes business sense for black people to coordinate CSI.'

At the time this profile was being written — shortly after the election and during a fragile transitional period — Radebe observed that some white CSI managers he knew were 'feeling somewhat awkward'. On the other hand, he says, 'I *know* the players — I grew up with them. It's part of the process of black economic empowerment.' Still, he feels, managing CSI successfully is getting harder: 'With all the changes, it's a different ball game. There are new players and complex decision-making structures — and it's a new country.'

Southern Life Foundation
Great Westerford
Rondebosch 7700
Phone: (021) 658-0327
Fax: (021) 685-4935

Summary:
The tightly-run Southern Life Foundation prefers to target its spending to help launch worthy organisations or support some of the special projects these groups run and then steps back as other funders step in. Some of these projects have grown substantially, such as the Triple Trust Organisation (TTO), now a sophisticated NGO which offers full training, support and consulting to develop small businesses. The Foundation makes a point of explaining its activities in a quarterly newsletter that circulates within the company; the newsletter also encourages employees to get involved in community projects.

*   *   *

The Southern Life Foundation is an interesting example of how a small CSI programme uses limited resources to have great impact. With a staff of just two — Executive Director Virginia Ogilvie Thompson and her assistant — the Foundation specialises in four areas: pre-school education training, teacher upgrading, job creation and health (with an emphasis on preventative rather than curative medicine).

Ogilvie Thompson is especially proud of instances in which trustees have authorised start-off funds to help launch new projects (such as the Alexandra AIDS Action community education initiative; the first phase of an ethnobotany research programme at the University of Natal's Institute of Natural Resources; and the TTO) and then watched them grow as other funders have come in.

In several cases, Southern Life then ended its support in order to direct its resources elsewhere. Or it directs funding towards specific projects, such as the numeracy workbooks produced by an NGO called COUNT; Southern used to fund its newsletter but decided to turn its attention toward a new workbook series. 'It's very nice to start something, to be instrumental in setting something up and then leave,' she says.

The Foundation was established in 1991, the centenary year of The Southern Life Association Limited. The company's CSI activi-

Company profiles

ties were previously coordinated by the corporate communications
department. Salaries and overheads are managed by a separate
department at Southern Life, and the company pays all administrative expenses and salaries so that the income generated from two
investment funds can be used entirely for grants.

The Foundation's seven trustees decide how much money will
be spent, but the Foundation will not disclose this sum. 'As the
fourth largest life assurance company in the country, our total dis-
bursements are minnow-like compared to Liberty Life, but when
taken as a percentage of dividend our figure is high,' Ogilvie
Thompson comments.

Although many firms base their CSI priorities on the tax relief
they get for donations (particularly to tertiary education), the
Southern Life Foundation has invested more of its education budget on pre-school programmes, many of which are not exempt. 'The
iniquities of the laws of South Africa have meant that many pre-
school projects do not qualify for deductions, but we went for them
anyway,' Ogilvie Thompson notes.

At this writing, Ogilvie Thompson pointed out that the
Foundation was supporting projects on a short-term basis while
waiting for the new government to announce its plans. If, for example, a national policy is announced that will funnel major state
investment into early childhood education, the Foundation may
change its focus. However, 'I don't think the government will have
sufficient money,' Ogilvie Thompson says, and she expects that
CSI departments will continue to have an important proactive role
to play.

In any case, flexibility is the name of the game for many CSI
practitioners these days, and while Southern did not support peace
initiatives in its earlier days, it funded the first two episodes of the
Peace Cafe television shows and donated money to the Family
Institute, which counsels families victimised by violence.

Similarly, concerned with black empowerment, Southern sought
to support a black-run educational support organisation after feeling
that another group that had received funds was "too white". But the
organisation that had been identified had too many problems and
was not working out. 'It's no good being over-enthusiastic about a
very small organisation if it doesn't have capacity to deliver services,' she cautions.

On the other hand, identifying what constitutes successful projects and which are failures can be difficult. 'You can't expect to
win them all. I might think a project is a flop but the sponsoring

organisation might like it,' Ogilvie Thompson says. But when she sees a project that works, she tries to find ways to enable it to carry on, expand and be replicated elsewhere.

Getting the message across

One way to do that is through publicity. So, in addition to an annual review, the Foundation publishes a quarterly in-house newsletter, *Foundation Focus,* which reports on projects it supports. Without a huge investment of money, the newsletter promotes good projects, examines how and why they work, and disseminates the information within the company and to other CSI departments and community programmes. The newsletter is one way to "multiply" Southern's work.

Another is for Ogilvie Thompson to sit on the boards of projects to which Southern has given support, so that she can have advisory input, keep abreast of developments and ensure that Southern's donation is being used correctly. This is different from the direct involvement practised by the Gencor and Nedcor trusts, but the Southern Life Foundation does not have the capacity to be so hands-on. Ogilvie Thompson is also 'keen for employee involvement to increase' — another way to enlarge the CSI "pie". 'We'd like employees to get involved in leadership development and in their community,' she says. To that end, the Southern Life Foundation gave a small grant to an employees' group.

In addition, she enlists the help of company accountants to assist organisations the Foundation supports in keeping their books. Southern's Johannesburg office allowed one of its black accountants to work with the Bophelo-Impilo Community Association, a grassroots group on whose board Ogilvie Thompson sits. (See Bophelo-Impilo Community Association Profile on p151.)

Supporting capacity building

The Southern Life Foundation was a funder of the NGO Programme at the University of Cape Town, which provides social sciences students with technical and management skills to run NGOs effectively. In the pilot programme launched in 1993, four NGOs became part of the training curriculum. The course includes workshops in which corporate managers "loan" their expertise. For instance, some Southern employees donated a few hours to share their management expertise with NGO staff members.

Finally, a valuable way to "multiply" CSI is to recognise employees who give time to their communities. To this end — and totally separate from the Foundation — Southern's Employee Benefits division awards the employee who has done the most.

Using a board to spread its clout
One of the interesting features of the Southern Life Foundation is the make-up of its board. While most board members of the trusts profiled in this book are executives from the sponsoring company (the Colgate-Palmolive Foundation is an exception), Southern's six trustees come from the corporate and community sectors.

Two are from the company: the chairman, Neal Chapman, and Arie van der Zwan, Southern's executive director for strategic services. The others are Professor Francis Wilson, Anastasia Thula, Sam Montsie, chairman of Thebe Investments, and Dr Nthato Motlana, South Africa's best-known black physician and a businessman who has pioneered several corporate buyouts by black investment consortia. Dr Motlana has remained on the Foundation's board even though he resigned from Southern Life's board in 1993 when an investment consortium he heads won control of rival firm Metropolitan Life, South Africa's fifth largest life assurer.

Knowing one's limitations
Despite the Southern Life Foundation's achievements, there are times when Ogilvie Thompson feels daunted by the endless needs. 'You have to "school" yourself to handle this job. Solomon himself couldn't put the thing right,' she says. Nor can funders whose chief task is to make grants. 'Each and every South African who has a job is privileged and must make sure to make some type of contribution. Sometimes you get desperately depressed. We have to be made of iron not to be. The joy of children from good projects is infectious. You get a lot of joy. But you also get depressed. We have to turn down more than half the requests.'

During its brief existence, the Southern Life Foundation has refined its giving strategy to spread out its benefits. Except for having been a charter donor to the JET (through a separate gift from the parent company), it never gives more than R100 000 to one project in one financial year, but the Foundation remains loyal to projects that it believes have real impact.

This policy coincides with statements by some NGOs that donors should not arbitrarily stop funding them because of a self-imposed time limit on grants if the recipient provides an essential service. So, for example, the READ Educational Trust receives an ongoing grant from Southern. But in line with its project-oriented strategy, Southern targets specific programmes, such as READ's Village Bus and Story Packs (see READ Educational Trust Profile on p176).

Among the projects Ogilvie Thompson feels proudest of supporting are the TTO in Cape Town and the Bophelo-Impilo Community Association in Johannesburg. (See the Profiles on p187 and p151.)

TTO trains unemployed people in basic business and marketing skills so that they can start their own businesses. Its white founders had backgrounds in accounting and manpower training and were just starting out when she heard about it through the CSI grapevine. The Southern Life Foundation was the first donor for an initial training programme. TTO is now a sophisticated NGO — almost a big business in its own right — which receives funding from many sources, including the Independent Development Trust, the Joint Education Trust and foreign donors. 'I have no hesitation to help pilot something and then others take it up. That's my greatest job satisfaction,' states Ogilvie Thompson.

Bophelo-Impilo, started by a group of black women in Soweto, now hosts a range of projects, including vegetable gardens, skills upgrading classes for domestic workers and child-minding training schemes. Its centrepiece is a community school which occupies the building of a formerly white school and has classes from pre-kindergarten through matric. It lacks the slickness of TTO but the women who run it are dedicated to their community, accountable to donors and its board, and can identify local needs and develop appropriate programmes.

What impressed Ogilvie Thompson about each group is its strong internal leadership, sharply defined goals and a determination to see them through. In addition, each is transparent about how it works.

Since working for The Southern, which she joined in 1988, Ogilvie Thompson has been heartened by the growing diversity of the forms and nature of leadership in South Africa's development community. 'There's a much greater awareness of the "imperative necessity" these days,' she finds. 'More companies and individuals are getting involved, as part of the need for more democratic involvement. The element of patronage is beginning to fall away.'

Standard Bank Foundation
PO Box 312
Johannesburg 2000
Phone: (011) 636-2978
Fax: (011) 636-1858

Summary:

The Standard Bank Foundation, which runs the company's CSI, operates within the bank's group communications division and coordinates some of its activities with its marketing department. Don Macey, who heads the Foundation, anticipates an even greater synergy in the future, which will also include tie-ins with human resources programmes. Major trends at the Foundation include more transparency (the Foundation publishes a social report which now includes social spending information), decentralisation of some CSI activities to regional offices, and fairer racial representation in the grantmaking process, which, with the exception of very large donations, is currently decided by a six-member committee that includes four black people.

* * *

It's probably no coincidence that in 1993, a time when many companies were giving higher profiles to their CSI programmes, the Standard Bank Foundation named Don Macey, a career communicator, to run it. Associated with the bank since 1963, Macey has made it his business to promote the Foundation's activities, and he was very willing to answer every question posed for this profile with almost minute detail, and then to add information that was not solicited. 'What has emerged since I started this job is a more holistic approach to CSI,' Macey said. 'We can't operate in isolation any more.'

Furthermore, Macey envisions CSI, which is budgeted at about R8 million annually (*not* including a six-year R30 million commitment by the bank to JET), as much more than making grants to community groups. He sees it as 'a positive investment' which also includes improving employee well being and lobbying to undo harmful legislation, such as laws that limit business operations in black townships. (No other company discussed the potential lobbying role of CSI.) What Macey calls Standard's internal CSI — spending on employee needs — is funded separately.

At one point, the Standard Foundation was developing an awards programme to honour NGOs that provided the best services and had an excellent personnel development policy and budget management. Tentatively planned as a co-sponsorship with the *Sowetan* newspaper, the project was put on hold when it appeared that much of the funding that used to go to NGOs was likely to be channelled into government for the RDP, and that the government would assign NGOs to certain projects.

As an alternative, the Foundation was considering an awards programme to honour the best educational outreach and bridging initiatives. 'We have identified educational outreach as particularly important at this juncture,' says Macey, 'since these endeavours help "level the playing fields" on the educational front.'

Out of the chairman's office

In 1974, following a trend among larger companies, Standard's CSI programme was moved into corporate public affairs from the chairman's office, where it had been a 'cosy, close executive floor operation'. But until 1985, when the Foundation was formed, it was mainly reactive to appeals rather than proactive, and operated on a modest budget. The Foundation itself is made up of two trusts, one for charitable giving and the other for education. They are separate because of South African tax laws that provide relief for educational donations. (The Foundation receives about 1 percent of post-tax profit from each business unit of Standard Bank.)

Nowadays the Foundation has four full-time staff: Macey, two foundation assistants and a secretary, plus a part-time Foundation assistant — a black Wits University social sciences graduate, who is being "mentored" to work in communications and personnel and to liaise with communities on the Foundation's behalf. The staff sifts through 20 to 30 appeals that arrive daily and conduct a complex follow-up procedure to monitor how funded projects perform. (Applicants must complete a standardised form when requesting funds. This procedure makes processing them much easier for staff.) An advisory board of prominent people from the black community meets quarterly to advise the Foundation on trends when they make policy.

Previously, a board of trustees — all white men — signed off on all projects. Under a new arrangement, Macey and his colleague, Sarah Nortje, work closely with a committee made up of the Indian manager of Standard Bank's Hillbrow branch and three black managers, to approve donations of up to R15 000. Grants up to R25 000 must be signed off by the Group Communications General Manager, and larger sums go to the Board of Trustees.

The Foundation is encouraging more employee involvement, in part by highlighting Standard's CSI programmes in its in-house corporate newsletter and by devolving some of its giving to its regions. Its six regional public relations offices (three of which are headed by women) get CSI budgets of more than R100 000 each. 'Corporate citizenship is a two-way flow,' states Macey.

An integrated approach to CSI

As part of its strategy to be more open — an approach Macey thinks is good for business — the Standard Bank Foundation now publishes a six-page social report which contains some financial details but remains sketchy compared to the more thorough social reports of the Liberty Life Foundation, Pick 'n Pay and the Toyota Foundation. Macey expects future reports to contain more details on contributions and grants, and a closer alignment to the RDP.

However, its social report, like Pick 'n Pay's, describes human resources programmes, employee relations, workplace diversity and employee involvement. This last item is meant to encourage more workplace participation, both on an individual basis and in teams. The programme is still new for Standard Bank, but reflects what the report says is 'in line with global trends, and recognises the need for effective employee involvement in decision-making'. The company honours employee teamwork with the Managing Director's Teamwork Award. And unlike companies which keep internal and community concerns separate, Macey expects increased synergy between the two.

The report makes a brief reference to the company's need to be 'environmentally responsible'. This is a concern that Macey believes will become more important in years to come. 'One woman at the company said we have to go black before we go green, but I disagree,' he says.

Marketing and CSI: A constant wrangle

An important operational change at the Foundation is that it carries all of its own costs, making it more independent of the company. 'This is a trend worldwide,' Macey notes. 'The Foundation cannot be coerced by our marketing people into making grants.'

Even so, the Foundation and the bank's marketing department do coordinate some projects. For instance, the Standard Bank National Arts Festival in Grahamstown is funded by the marketing department, but the Foundation underwrites a training programme in arts administration for talented black candidates. And while marketing sponsors tennis tournaments, the Foundation funds township tennis training programmes. This is a good process, says Macey, who foresees 'a day not too far away when all of these things — human resources, marketing and CSI — can come under one roof'. As it is, the company's education and training division already donate time and personnel to some remedial education programmes that the Foundation supports.

Standard Foundation's priorities
Education is a strong priority at Standard Bank Foundation. In 1994, it represented 70 percent of the budget, while the remaining 30 percent was earmarked for charity, welfare, arts and culture and the environment. With the exception of Standard's donation to the Joint Education Trust, the largest donations range up to R130 000, and represent a handful of grants.

In 1993, the largest grant recipients included The Valley Trust (R120 000); Ntataise Rural Preschool Trust; Supplementary Education Programme (SUPEDI), which runs Saturday schools for students in Standards Three to Seven (R127 000); the Star Schools, since renamed the Standard Bank ReWrite School (R130 000); Junior Achievement Entrepreneurial training for students in Standards Eight and Nine, which helps them set up small businesses selling T-shirts and other items (R89 000 in 1993); the Model United Nations at Wits University (R72 000); Molteno (R75 000) and the Education Support Services Trust.

One of Macey's favourite projects is Creches Care, a programme which brings well-equipped "mobile" creches, in renovated buses and with qualified teachers, to black townships to give special preparation in school readiness. Since 1991 the Foundation has given Creches Care an annual donation to cover running costs, raising it from an initial grant of R20 000 in 1991 to R40 000 in 1994 (see Creches Care Profile on p158).

Vision for the future
As at other companies, Macey believes that Standard Bank will support a more visible, strategic role for the Foundation. 'Like public relations, social investment is becoming an element that senior management can't ignore,' he believes. 'Government can't meet most needs and we must try to address them.' CSI will represent a portion of Standard's RDP contribution.

To some extent, the appointment of a 30-year veteran from the bank to run Standard's CSI seems an odd move at a time when pressure is on to place a black person at the helm. But the decision seems to reflects the need to raise the Foundation's profile as it asserts itself as a separate entity, and Macey is superb at doing this. (In addition to his activities at the bank, he teaches public relations at Damelin College.) Macey makes a point of actively networking with his counterparts at other banks and at certain other companies, sometimes collaborating on projects. 'JCI has set a wonderful example in this regard,' he says.

It's important, says Macey, that each company develop a funding approach appropriate to its business. Mining houses are more likely to fund capital projects while banks may underwrite running costs. And if one finds a project that, in Macey's words, is 'a bad egg, we share that information with each other'. If Macey likes a project but cannot authorise the funding it needs, he may alert other funders to help out.

Macey admits a few shortfalls in his work: not enough time for site visits, especially to the educational bridging programmes to which the Foundation plans to increase funding, and perhaps not enough monitoring. Recipients are currently subject to an annual review. And few organisations get long-term grants, in order to avoid problems that may arise when money is given away and not accounted for.

Avoiding burnout

'Whenever we get together in a forum we all say we love our jobs but commiserate because of work pressures,' is how Macey describes meeting his colleagues. 'We all run very lean and we get tired.' Outside interests are important, and for Macey this includes his Damelin lecturing and serving as vice-chair of the Delta Environmental Centre. He also reads for Tape Aids for the Blind. 'I believe that every one of us should give a little of our time to some cause or community we believe in. We need voluntarism; it enriches us as well,' he says.

Toyota South Africa Foundation
PO Box 481
Bergvlei 2012
Phone: (011) 809-2486
Fax: (011) 444-6567

Summary:

Full disclosure is good for a company, the Toyota South Africa Foundation learned in 1993, when it got mostly positive feedback for publishing a Foundation report that includes a complete break-down of its CSI spending, along with projected budgets for 1994 and 1995. This was a breakthrough for South African CSI; no company until then had been so transparent. This step is part of a process to bring Toyota's CSI into the business mainstream. It includes a programme at head office that requires line managers to take part in community projects in Alexandra township, where many employees live, bringing their expertise to township organisations that can use in-kind help. Such involvement give managers a greater stake in community welfare when they see first-hand what employees who live in troubled areas must cope with.

* * *

The Toyota South Africa Foundation attracted attention within the CSI community in 1993 for its bold full-disclosure policy. That was when the Foundation published a report which not only described the projects it funds but listed spending on all of them, including projected spending in coming years. This was a dramatic change for Toyota's CSI, which was overhauled by group social investment manager Susan Smit, who joined the firm in 1990. Until then — as at many companies — CSI was mainly a cheque-writing exercise. 'When I started people were very uncertain about what CSI was,' says Smit. 'I just got a directive to start it up, but no one knew how. Over time it grew from being a distributor of funds to being very involved in capacity-building.'

As someone new to the field, Smit had to learn on the job — and without a support system to draw on, either at Toyota's Marketing division offices in Johannesburg, where she is based, or at its Durban operations. Eight thousand employees work at four divisions in Natal and another 1 300 are in Johannesburg. Three regional offices in Cape Town, Port Elizabeth and Bloemfontein employ fewer than 100 people.

CSI as an employee-empowering tool

A distinctive feature of Toyota's CSI is an employee involvement component run from its Johannesburg office. It requires divisional heads to support projects in nearby Alexandra township, where many employees live; managers are appraised in part on their community inputs. This strategy sensitises managers to community issues and the realities of employees' lives. Their assistance includes donating expertise along with goods and services such as stationery and printing.

For example, a division might focus on youth education and send employee volunteers to Alex on Saturdays to do tutoring. Or Toyota's public relations department may help groups prepare brochures and learn how to do publicity. There could also be entrepreneurship training. One such link-up is with the Alexandra Industrialists Association, a confederation of township entrepreneurs, to which the company has provided marketing and financial advice.

Funding structure

Most of Toyota's CSI funds comes from two sources: the Toyota Foundation, which represents about R5 million (provided in equal parts from Toyota Japan and Toyota South Africa) and the Toyota South Africa Donations Committee, which in 1994 had R960 000 available. The Albert Wessels Trust, named for the first head of Toyota South Africa, also provides funds. In late 1994, Toyota Japan placed a further R2 million into a trust whose interest is designated for CSI.

The Foundation has a board of trustees chaired by Professor A C Nkabinde, retired rector of the University of Zululand. Other trustees include educationist Professor J P de Lange and members of the Wessels family. A 10-member Toyota Donations Committee meets four times a year to make major funding decisions. The committee consists of managers and employees, mainly union members. Smit can approve donations ranging from R500 to R1 000. Although trade union members and other employees may propose, discuss and take part in projects, they currently lack decision-making power on who gets funds, a situation Smit hopes will change.

The full Foundation report, Smit's idea, will be published annually. In addition to CSI reporting, the first report described programmes to assist black entrepreneurship, including the awarding of Toyota franchises, and employee housing and bursaries for employees' children. Future editions will include more information on "internal" CSI, such as a creche the company is building in Natal for employees' children. CSI information is also reported in Toyota's in-house newsletters and a twice-yearly report to employees, recently introduced at the company. Toyota's in-house monthly magazine usually has some reporting on CSI.

Toyota Teach

Toyota's biggest investment by far is its R8 million donation to 'Toyota Teach', a pilot teacher upgrading programme in Natal that builds instructional skills in science and maths for students in Standards Two to Five (see the Toyota Teach Profile on p184.) Most such programmes target high school students, but the planners of Toyota Teach felt that it was essential to focus on younger students in black schools, who are often bypassed for supplementary science and maths programmes, and, as a result, lack key skills by the time they reached high school.

Now in its first stage of evaluation, Toyota Teach has drawn extensively on the resources of several universities and NGOs, who devised a unique collaborative approach to programme development. Although it was 'helluva difficult to get the NGOs to work together at first', Smit recalls, they 'have now developed a good relationship'.

Other major funded projects include the motor mechanic training programme at the Alexandra Career-Directed Centre and Alex San Kopano, a community centre that offers many social services programmes.

More than writing cheques

Toyota's project involvement consists of far more than cheque-writing. 'I've never left a project,' says Smit. 'Money is just part of what projects need. It's also love and assistance and help and support. Holly Luton [at Alex San Kopano] started a sewing project but needed cloth. We helped with the cloth and then sold some of the garments to Toyota people. When the centre wanted people to give instruction about how engines work, we got our people who know about them to do it.'

Toyota was not one of the larger funders of the Alexandra Career-Directed Centre, but, through Smit's interventions, has been one of the most involved, helping to sort out problems as they arise, and the staff know her well. But at a reception to mark the centre's opening, Toyota was not listed among the donor companies. Such donor "exclusiveness" bothers her, especially since the sponsors have not made return visits. 'We always send someone in to see how our projects work,' Smit points out. 'If we don't get feedback on something, we find out what's going on.'

As with most CSI programmes, Smit fields funding requests all the time. Guidelines are minimal; Toyota has no application form, although Smit has examined models from Nedcor and South African Breweries. At this writing, Toyota was only funding projects in areas where employees live. When requests show good potential, she invites applicants to see her, or she and an associate (shop stewards who do project evaluation) visit the project to assess the role Toyota might play.

An outsider? Or perhaps not . . .

Smit is unusual as an Afrikaner woman in a field where most of the work targets black communities. Increasingly, new openings in CSI are being reserved for black candidates. In an earlier discussion about Toyota's CSI, Smit had said confidently that a black person *should* have her job. She now says she is not so sure: 'It is certainly true that black people know black culture best, but blacks can also be very hard on black people.'

She also notes that some black people may use CSI for political reasons and lose the objectivity required to run a programme properly. 'One guy wanted to do CSI so bad because he could feel that he would have a lot of power,' she says. 'I believe that the synergies between whites and blacks are fantastic. CSI can't be run only by blacks or only by whites. And blacks don't yet have the skills to do it.'

After having run a virtually one-woman show (with one full-time secretary), Smit put this "synergy" into practice in mid-1994, when Toyota authorised the appointment of a full-time social development officer to assist her. She recruited Andrew Maluleke, a shop steward, for the post; he had already investigated and evaluated many projects, knows Alexandra very well, is a good report writer and learner, and works well with people, Smit says.

'It's a definite affirmative action appointment,' she adds, noting that it could lead to a line position. (On her own part, Smit envisions that her job will eventually be held by a black Toyota employee — possibly Maluleke — and that she will move into another area of human resources, into which Toyota's CSI is slotted, although the programme runs independently of other human resources activities.)

How the job has changed

Smit recalls how hard her job was when she started and finds that with experience it has become easier. Yet 'the momentum and pressure from groups to help make it harder,' she adds. 'You must do lots of reading and research and constant networking. I love my job — I love people. I wanted to do something to change what was happening in South Africa, to change the minds of people in the company and communities. I'm dedicated and enthusiastic and love what I do.'

This brings Smit to explain the qualities she thinks CSI professionals need. 'You have to have a social investment heart, a caring attitude for people, not a cold clinical heart,' she suggests. 'You can teach all the other skills but not how to really care. You need to be dedicated, committed and have staying power. People get disillusioned if a project isn't finalised within two months. You need to be persistent — it can take a year or two to get off the ground. Then the excitement and satisfaction are extraordinary.' Good communications and writing skills are a key part of the job.

Smit agrees with suggestions that CSI practitioners be trained and accredited. Such training would teach not just how to be a donor but also a provider of capacity-building; how to write objective project evaluations and recommendations; how to judge projects appropriately; and how to plan CSI from a strategic business perspective.

In addition, Smit believes that CSI should include internal activities as well as community involvement and must therefore be recognised as a genuine business function, possibly aligned with the company's Employee Assistance Programme.

New directions

Like her activist counterparts, Smit is optimistic about new directions in CSI, which she says Toyota calls 'social development' in order to accommodate RDP guidelines. She anticipates more, not less, company involvement. 'We're moving into a new era and CSI has to change. And you have to be flexible. If the government launches into education, we'd move elsewhere and won't overspend in one area.'

Warner-Lambert Pharmaceutical Company
Private Bag X6
Tokai 7966
Phone: (021) 710-4111
Fax: (021) 710-4900

Summary:

Warner-Lambert was a long-time signatory to the Sullivan Principles and their successor, the Statement of Principles, and consistently earned a top Category I rating. With the dropping of trade sanctions and the scrapping of the code, the company has joined other US-owned firms in South Africa by reducing its social investment spending to what it says is a more reasonable level and targeting it more closely to business needs. However, it is retaining some features of the code, especially the section that refers to employee participation in community development projects. Though relatively small, Warner-Lambert has taken a leadership role in the Western Cape by helping to initiate a social investment association which enables local companies to network with each other and, in some cases, collaborate on projects. This is an especially useful way for smaller companies to become involved in CSI.

*   *   *

While some US-owned companies in South Africa say they don't expect to change their CSI significantly now that the Sullivan Code and its successor, the Statement of Principles, which monitored US social investment in South Africa, have been scrapped, Warner-Lambert is frank about its own planned changes. Social spending *will* go down, according to Public Affairs Manager Lutfia Vayej, from the previously mandated minimum of 12 percent of payroll in order to earn a top rating (which Warner-Lambert consistently did), to an amount it considers more "reasonable". This could be as much as 50 percent less of the R4,1 million that the company spent on CSI in 1993.

Under the Sullivan Code, Warner-Lambert prepared an annual social report to be audited by a US consultant for a rating. A new report, *Warner-Lambert Social Responsibility Review, 1990-1994*, was being prepared when this interview took place.

In addition, Warner-Lambert is in the process of revamping its approach to CSI to bring it more into line with business needs while simultaneously addressing key aspects of the government's RDP.

Rather than having to spread its activities over a wide range of areas, the company will engage in projects that are more market-related and can generate publicity by drawing attention to the company's involvement and participation in development.

Its new mission statement lists its primary focus on "the upliftment of disadvantaged communities through the provision of education [particularly non-formal education, teacher development and pre-school programmes], training, basic primary health care and the reconstruction, development and economic growth of these communities".

'It makes good business sense to link CSI to business needs, and we can do this without being restricted by the Sullivan code,' says Vayej. For example, the company might choose a theme around which to promote its CSI — and its products. In another instance, to help the confectionery division get more of its products into the black consumer market, Warner-Lambert might support NGOs that sponsor job creation projects and set up distribution centres and spaza shops in townships that would sell company products. 'This would have been a no-no under the Sullivan Code. The code was very specific about not allowing companies to exploit their involvement in social responsibility activities for business activities,' explains Vayej.

The company, a wholly-owned division of US pharmaceutical firm Warner-Lambert with 400 employees in South Africa, with facilities nationwide, consists of the Parke-Davis ethical division, the Parke-Med generic division, an over-the-counter division called Parke-Davis Health Care, and a confectionery division (including the brand names Trident, Hall's and Clorets). The company is putting new emphasis on products related to primary health care, in line with the new government's thrust on address basic health needs which were not adequately attended to under the "old" regime.

Encouraging local partnerships

What stands out about Warner-Lambert is the extent to which it has led the effort in the Western Cape to encourage networking with other companies. Such networking serves to promote information-sharing and project collaboration. Around 1988 (when Vayej joined the company), Warner-Lambert launched a social responsibility awards programme to urge non-signatory South African companies to get involved in community projects.

The awards were divided into three categories depending on the type of company: multinational; a South African company with more than than 100 employees; and a company with fewer than 100 employees. To enter, a company had to complete a questionnaire that asked about its housing, education and community development programmes — criteria that Signatory companies had come to know very well.

Two years later, the competition was replaced with a programme to form a regional CSI network. This effort began with a workshop on CSI strategies, especially for smaller companies with limited resources. The workshop served as the incubator for the Social Investment Association (SIA) of the Western Cape. Warner-Lambert, a founding member, provides it with extensive administrative support, an office, a meeting room, photocopying facilities and materials for its quarterly newsletter. The company funds the salary of a full-time coordinator who schedules meetings, liaises with the SIA's subcommittees and member companies, organises workshops and seminars and edits the newsletter. In addition, the SIA has created a database of local NGOs.

One of the SIA's subcommittees, chaired by the CSI representative from Safmarine, coordinates the Community Action Network (CAN), made up of about 20 companies involved in the construction of a business "hive" in the township of Khayelitsha.

The subcommittee negotiated for property, located volunteer architects to design the hive, and recruited volunteer engineers and land surveyors to do groundwork. At this writing, the project proposal and survey had been completed and was to be submitted to local community committees for their scrutiny and approval. (Another 'CAN' links 30 companies in Gauteng, with Safmarine's regional office acting as faciliator.)

Warner-Lambert's CSI is run by its public affairs department and involves three people. Vayej, who also holds the company's public affairs portfolio, says that CSI takes up 80 percent of her time. The others include an administrative assistant and a public affairs officer who divides her time between overseeing some of the social responsibility projects, including site visits, and administering Warner-Lambert's internal communications portfolio. On a voluntary basis, employees, including shop stewards, participate in project grant decisions.

Ample employee involvement
However, employee involvement — spurred on in part by an employee appraisal system which requires each department to take part in community projects — is ample, although Vayej is sceptical

about evaluation systems that prompt employees to get involved only to improve their job rating. (This system was part of the Sullivan Code.) But she believes that the company's small size makes employee involvement easier to coordinate.

For instance, the company's medical department has "adopted" a local pre-school and the National Cancer Association's Philani Cancer Education Project in the Western Cape, and pharmacists, secretaries and formulation scientists volunteer in a cancer awareness programme that targets black women.

The bulk of Warner-Lambert's CSI programmes are based in the Western Cape. Many are health-related, although job creation is also a priority. Donations often include medicine as well as funds. Among Vayej's favourite projects is CRIC (Career Research and Information Centre), a career guidance and resource centre that arranges student visits to companies and on-site internships. Warner-Lambert was one of its first funders.

Another favourite is the South African Christian Leadership Association (SACLA), which runs a primary health care clinic in Crossroads township, offers health worker training, provides a strong rehabilitation programme for stroke victims and physically disabled people, makes home visits, and provides ante-natal and post-natal care. It also funds its community health worker training programme and sponsors bursaries for pharmaceutical studies, and Warner-Lambert donates medicine.

And the company underwrites a rural-based AIDS education programme run by an NGO called Phambili, which trains mothers and traditional healers.

To monitor its CSI giving, Warner-Lambert insists — 'if possible', Vayej notes — on progress reports, annual reports, quarterly updates and regular meetings. On occasion, she or a colleague will become a trustee or committee member of a grantee organisation and make regular visits. Officials in the company's finance department often provide business advice and assistance to small business projects.

Warner-Lambert used to support cooperative businesses, but found that the people involved often did not know how to market their products. In one case, the company donated sewing machines to a project that "oversewed" and could not sell its wares. To avoid such mistakes, Warner-Lambert now prefers to work with NGOs that offer training in accounting and marketing.

A background in teaching and counselling helps with job effectiveness

A journalist by training, Vayej had teaching and guidance counselling experience before she joined Warner-Lambert in 1988. So her background combined writing and working with people. But she was not entirely prepared for the frequency with which she must 'face things you don't necessarily want to see: poverty, depression, homelessness. But you have to do it to have an understanding of what's going on. You need to be very clued up and be assertive and, most important, have the right personality. You have to represent company and also be yourself. It can be tiresome." But she wouldn't want to work elsewhere in the company. "I'm not a real corporate animal," she admits. "Our marketing people are largely occupied with the business side of things and they don't have time to think about CSI. I'm caught up in the real world through what I do."

Despite the pressures of her work, Vayej (who went on maternity leave in late 1994) is optimistic about the direction of CSI. "There's suddenly a seriousness now," she says. "Many companies that were not involved before are being asked to act affirmatively in everything they do. Some are showing up at meetings, seminars and discussions on development strategies. They realise that it makes good business sense to get involved and that the private sector has an important role to play in the reconstruction of our country." But confusion about new tax laws and legislation worry Vayej, who is concerned that CSI programmes could end up duplicating some of the programmes the new government has in mind. And she also worries that good NGOs, particularly the hundreds of small ones who are doing essential community work, might be forced to shut down if they do not get support.

PART III

Project profiles

CHAPTER 6

Project profiles

African Institute of Technology
c/o The Matla Trust
PO Box 7748
Johannesburg 2000
Phone: (011) 836-8061
Fax: (011) 838-1910

In early 1994, the Lotus Trust's Mackie McLeod spoke proudly of the achievements of the African Institute of Technology (AIT), a black-led computer training project which Lotus, along with other computer software and hardware firms in South Africa, had helped to fund. But when I visited AIT a few weeks after the elections, its premises at Shell House in downtown Johannesburg were nearly deserted and training had ground to a halt.

AIT's difficulties were attributed in part to the lack of long-term strategic planning which some NGOs fail to undertake, but in some respect, it was a casualty of the transition to democracy. Whatever the reason, the AIT experience is an example of how a narrow programme that has not been planned for the long term — or for contingencies — can cause a good programme to go awry. But all is not lost.

AIT, which was formed by Matla Trust, was a good idea. It aimed to be a black-led training institution to provide high-level computer training to NGOs and other institutions. Such training is important, particularly in giving good role models to black youngsters seeking to improve their technical skills. At the outset its principal client was the staff at the African National Congress's Shell House headquarters, where AIT occupied part of a floor. But at a certain point, almost all the targeted ANC staff had been trained, and AIT had not done a sufficient job in advertising its services beyond the ANC. Then, after the elections, three of AIT's core staffers joined the new government.

As a project of the Matla Trust, AIT will continue, although at the time I spoke with director Colin de Vos, it was being restructured. It has relocated from Shell House to the building where Matla is based.

South Africa badly needs the type of high-technology training that AIT was preparing to offer, so it will be important to see what the next moves will be. McLeod suggests that the Lotus Trust may take over the management of AIT to use it as an in-town site for its training programmes. This would be an excellent solution since it's much easier for the many AIT students who live in outlying townships to get to central Johannesburg than to Lotus's offices in Rivonia. And it would be more economical to manage.

In any case, funders involved with computer training must never sit on their laurels; when a project they fund is stalled, the equipment they donated quickly becomes outdated, as was the case at AIT in mid-1994: rooms were filled with never-opened boxes of software that had already become obsolete. AIT's other core corporate sponsors included ISG, WordPerfect and Microsoft.

BMW Early Learning Centre
c/o BMW SOUTH AFRICA
PO Box 2955
Pretoria 0001
Phone: (012) 529-2753
Fax: (012) 541-9040

You have to walk some distance along a path adjacent to the employee parking area at BMW before you reach the Early Learning Centre, but the rambustious noise of children playing reassures you that you're heading in the right direction.

A playground in front of the centre is packed with three- to six-year-olds who are being watched by a young assistant teacher named Freddy, the centre's only male staffer. Inside the centre, which has one huge open room and several partitioned spaces, as well as a kitchen and a few small offices, teachers work with groups of children on art projects, read stories, lead music sessions and play games. At the same time, the centre encourages more free-spirited children to go off on their own, exploring how to make pictures at the painting easel, dressing dolls in the doll corner or playing with blocks.

The day I was there, two were chattering away on a toy wall telephone. For teacher-directed activities, the children are divided into groups identified as the Buffaloes, the Elephants, the Rhinos and the Hippos. These groups occasionally take field trips to the zoo, museums and recreation centres, places they might never visit otherwise.

My visit took place a few weeks after South Africa's first non-racial election, and there was a display of the voting patterns of the group. Despite the children's young age, they knew about the elections because of their parents' acute interest, explained principal Sue Rosie, who left a position on the faculty of Soweto College of Education to run the centre. 'Children's families are very politically aware and they pass it on to their kids,' she said. They had a mock election in the centre and had 26 percent spoiled ballots — a high percentage that Rosie attributes to having granted three-year-olds the vote.

The centre, which opened in 1989, runs five days a week from 6:30 am until 5:00 pm. Children can have breakfast, a mid-morning snack, lunch and a late afternoon snack. Parents may visit whenever they want. A Saturday Youth Development Programme offers courses to more than 100 teenagers in technical and life skills.

In a previous incarnation, the programme targeted a few talented students and gave them bursaries to attend private schools, but the company felt it was more appropriate to help more students succeed in the schools they already attend. (The centre also used to be open after-hours, including weekends, for what Rosie calls Parent Interest Development Groups. These aimed to teach cooking, baking, gardening, public speaking and other skills that parents requested, but the groups were on hold when we met.)

Employee support has kept the centre going since it opened. 'We thought employee funds would peter out and we would then explore other options, but we've never had to,' says Rosie. 'The school is equipped exclusively through the fundraising raffle.' BMW pays the salaries of five teaching staff, while the raffle covers the salaries of three cleaners.

The raffle, run by employees at BMW plants, takes place every two months, with a R10 000 first prize, a R3 000 second prize and seven R1 000 third prizes. This means that R20 000 must be raised just to cover prizes. Each ticket costs R20 and sellers, who by now have developed a regular customer base, have 50 tickets in a book. For every book sold, the sellers get one free ticket. Overheads are negligable and the only cost to run the raffle is to print books. But the raffle itself is critical to cover costs. Parents pay only R115 per month to enrol their children at the centre, but the actual cost is R400 per month per child.

The raffle has always been a huge success, and the reason is clear-cut, Rosie suggests: 'The buyers know the money is going into something they benefit from.' Many parents are assembly line workers who, notes Rosie, are 'passionate about getting education for their children and will make sacrifices'. In fact, employee funds are now being used to cover the costs of erecting a new building, across from the playground. It will accommodate older children, although some projects will continue to mix children of different ages, because Rosie believes older children can serve as a teaching resource for younger ones.

A new centre for 50 children is being built at BMW's Midrand headquarters. It was scheduled to open in early 1995.

What is it about BMW that made such employee input possible? And why aren't such employee initiatives taking place elsewhere? The reason may be a bit difficult to answer, but Rosie thinks it's not money but people.

Bophelo-Impilo Community Association
201 Sheffield House, 2nd floor
29 Kruis Street
Johannesburg 2001
Phone: (011)331-1052/4

Bophelo is a grassroots NGO started in 1982 by a group of Soweto women to provide services to their community. Its executive director, Anastasia Thula, is a trained community health nurse with strong organisational and leadership qualities plus a steely determination. (She is married to Gibson Thula, one of South Africa's leading black business figures.) One of her office assistants is a former domestic worker who carries out her job with pride and polish.

Bophelo and *Impilo* are Sotho and Nguni words for "health", which, Thula explained when I visited her office, signifies the organisation's vision of an approach to living. Thus the programme focuses on self-help projects for young people and senior citizens, but, most importantly, for women. These include a child-minding scheme started in 1979, the International Year of the Child. (Bophelo did not yet exist, but the child-minding programme provided the framework for the organisation to launch other projects.)

Among the other activities are a handicraft club; a bulk buying club; a vegetable gardens project; an upgrading programme for domestic workers to improve their general housekeeping skills; a family and citizens club for older people to pray, sing, do handiwork and cook together; a sewing club; a youth club and a catering organisation.

The centrepiece of Bophelo is the Bophelo-Impilo Community School in Mayfair, a 10-minute drive from its downtown Johannesburg office. The school started as a programme for school dropouts in the mid-1980s, when it was housed in a Diepkloof church. At that time many students had come from detention or were enrolled in the Streetwise programme for homeless children. The programme then grew to include a pre-school and after-school programmes for young adults.

In 1991 Bophelo convinced the DET to turn over a formerly all-white but then empty school in Mayfair for its use — the first such conversion in South Africa. On beautiful premises with a huge yard — a vast contrast to most school facilities in black townships — it now teems with black children (and a handful of whites), many from poor homes.

The school is tightly run by several committees including curriculum, budget and finance, as well as an active parents group. It also has a board of governors and board of trustees to ensure accountability. School fees were R10 per month in its first year but are now R900 per year at the pre-school, R1 500 at the middle school and R2 000 at the high school, raised in part to pay better teacher salaries. (Some bursaries are available for students from poor families.) Although Thula notes that some CSI managers were sceptical of Bophelo's ability to run the school, the organisation has recruited an able core administrative and teaching staff. 'It's an RDP prototype,' Thula says.

Despite being based in central Johannesburg, Bophelo lacks access to the types of computer networks that larger, more sophisticated NGOs take for granted, and Thula was unaware of the existence of the Development Resources Centre (DRC) that could provide her with information on possible new funding sources or training programmes that would benefit her staff. In any case, Bophelo runs on a shoestring and, for instance, would probably not be able to afford membership in SangoNet, the electronic NGO bulletin board that DRC spawned.

The walls of Bophelo's offices, which are based in the former premises of the South African Jewish Board of Deputies, are covered with handwritten posters and photographs illustrating its programmes. It is anything but slick, and Thula knows this. 'We're pure struggle by the grassroots, 'she makes clear. 'We make mistakes in front of Virginia [Ogilvie Thompson of the Southern Foundation, a long-time supporter of Bophelo-Impilo.]. We're on a learning curve.'

The women running Bophelo don't have sophisticated proposal writing and accounting skills, and this is where outside assistance, such as the "loaning" of Southern Life accountants comes in. However, a regular period of programme analysis, a thorough annual report and a board of advisers which includes outside experts, keeps Bophelo running smoothly and accountable to its donors.

Careers Resources Information Centre (CRIC)
PO Box 378
Athlone 7760
Phone: (021) 637-8040
Fax: (021) 633-9022

CRIC was founded in 1977, a direct response by grassroots activists to the education crisis in black South African schools that exploded one year earlier. Initially an information and training centre, it received grants from a handful of corporate donors, including Shell, Syfrets and Anglo American.

The leaders of the original organisation, says Tahir Salie, CRIC's executive director since 1987, 'were visionary. They saw that our work was key in contributing to economic growth.' And at a time when it was unpopular for such groups to do so, CRIC worked closely with the black school departments because they knew they had a valuable service to offer.

In time it became clear that there was a need to do more than provide information. So CRIC developed a training centre as well, to help teachers give career guidance and counselling to students. Eventually it went nationwide, with resource centres in the Free State and other often-neglected areas around South Africa, having impact, estimates Salie, on up to three million people. Nowadays, CRIC has a full-time staff of 27 and is also involved in international networks; Salie sits on the board of the International Association of Educational and Vocational Guidance, based in Northern Ireland.

CRIC offers more than on-site services; for users who cannot visit its centres, CRIC runs a correspondence service and produces print material and videos. These methods all aim to reach CRIC's target users, mainly very disadvantaged youth who have been marginalised by the system, although it also serves students from working-class homes who aspire to become middle class. Their parents may not be aware of opportunities for to further their children's education, and CRIC therefore provides a necessary service to them. CRIC is a 'critical component' of the RDP, according to Bernard Fanaroff, assistant to Jay Naidoo in developing a national RDP policy.

CRIC's Services Unit has six components: a careers library, on-site counselling, distance counselling, a work experience programme, educator training and development, and a variety of educational programmes. These include camps for participants in student representative councils who learn voter education, combating sexism and racism, making a career choice, conflict resolution and dealing with unemployment.

Teacher training and development is key to CRIC, and includes workshops and lectures to pre-service teachers at University of the Western Cape and University of Cape Town. In-service programmes provide workshops in developing a guidance curriculum, understanding the state's new Education Renewal Strategy, and presenting information on work and education.

Its media unit creates print and broadcast media, including a monthly programme on Radio Xhosa and a series of comics, posters and booklets, some of which were produced as a joint venture with *Upbeat* magazine.

A new Enterprise Education unit (EE) was launched in 1992 by CRIC in conjunction with the Career Information Centre in Durban and the Education Information Centre in Johannesburg. With the help of professional trainers, EE aims to enable young people between the ages of 18 to 25 to develop community projects based on their vocational, academic and personal interests.

These projects would help develop their skills in dealing with people with power, seeing through responsibilities, communicating, problem solving and improving technical and practical skills. EE was developed to address the lack of traditional jobs and the prospect of continued unemployment. It was still in the pilot phase when this profile was written.

Lastly, CRIC's Karoo Resource Centre offers services in rural areas of the Karoo, targeting 42 schools in 28 towns, and helping students with subject choice, choosing a career and study methods, bursaries and loans, matric exemption and different study institutions. However, literacy training needs are great in this region, and the centre helped set up an Independent Literacy Centre to train specialists.

New US and other investors don't know about CRIC, laments Salie, who is also seeking ways to generate income for the organisation as well as attract more donors. These could include contracting out its publications for a fee and asking higher prices for some of the products it sells. 'We're always torn about whether to donate our publications or charge something for them,' Salie admits.

**Centre for Advancement of Science and
Mathematics Education (CASME)**
PO Box 17112
Congella 4013
Phone: (031) 811-390
Fax: (031) 815-070

'It's all about teacher leadership' is how Stan Hardman summarises
CASME, the Centre for Advancement of Science and Mathematics
Education, whose resource centres Hardman oversees. The statement underlies the mission of CASME: to advance science and
maths education in South Africa through improving the skills of
maths and science teachers at secondary schools in black areas
whose population and resources are not apt to change dramatically
in the years ahead.

The statistics make CASME's mission compelling: at a time
when South Africa needs all the skilled technical personnel it can
get, 96 percent of its engineers and 89 percent of its scientists come
from the white population, while just one black student among
10 000 achieves a university entrance in maths and science. In
1985, these harsh facts drove Shell South Africa to launch the Shell
Maths and Science Programme, which was later renamed CASME
to reflect the fact that it has other significant funders, including
Eskom and the Independent Development Trust (although Shell
still funds almost half the budget) and a more comprehensive
programme.

These days CASME, based at the University of Natal, is so busy
and well-staffed that it is nearly bursting out of the building it occupies. Yet despite the urgent need for what it does, it is South
Africa's only programme offering in-service training for maths and
science secondary school teachers.

CASME's activities are mainly limited to KwaZulu/Natal,
although it has recently developed projects in Kroonstad in the Free
State and Witbank in the Eastern Transvaal. Its ongoing projects
include in-service courses in the physical and biological sciences as
well as mathematics; eight regional support centres in
KwaZulu/Natal and new ones in Kroonstad and Witbank; and support groups of teachers working on projects to which CASME
makes annual grants of R2 000 per subject interest group.

The resource centres provide meeting spaces for teachers,

courses in their subject areas, access to photocopying and videos, and courses in materials development, such as biology models and other visual aids for classroom instruction. As a result of transport difficulties getting to the centres, especially from rural areas, CASME is exploring ways to develop more school and community-based programmes.

In addition, CASME is trying to increase direct teacher involvement in curriculum and materials development. This more interactive approach aims to give teachers a greater sense of "ownership" of the programme and, CASME believes, will help make them better teachers. 'We want to create a cadre of black teachers in leadership positions, in the classroom, in the programmes and in the community,' Hardman explains.

There's considerable emphasis on new technologies as well. For instance, CASME's "Learning Radio" project helps students understand electronics by building a basic radio using inexpensive parts. CASME also supports a Computers in Schools project to promote technology use in education. Dozens of teachers are being taught basic computer skills.

But at CASME's core is *not* materials development but teacher development. Promoting teachers' technique and self-confidence is seen as an empowerment process in which teachers are encouraged to become more proactive, creative, responsible and self-assured. The process is not easy, since it challenges archaic pedagogical approaches that rely on rote learning and discouraging student participation.

CASME, in fact, dares teachers to become more independent and to challenge their students to see themselves as "stakeholders" in the learning process. CASME's science room awards programme helps move this process along. The awards honour the best science rooms teachers have developed. Judges visit participating schools and give all of them a judge's report and a small award, although the best ones get a main award.

A ceremony bringing all the teachers together highlights winning projects and gives teachers a sense of pride in their work. CASME also offers a Further Diploma Education programme consisting of accredited courses to advance teaching skills and credentials — and enable teachers to earn higher salaries.

CASME is an obvious RDP prototype, and its model is being explored for national application. Director John Volmink sits on the ANC's task team on science and maths education, and CASME is part of a programme funded by the Independent Development Trust to explore the impact of teacher upgrading programmes (including Toyota Teach) at 1 000 schools nationwide, of which 30 percent are secondary and 70 percent primary, or, looked at another way, are 30 percent urban and 70 percent rural.

Does CASME work? An evaluation of matric results at selected schools showed that students taught by CASME-trained teachers performed twice as well as those whose teachers had not gone through the programme, 'so we believe CASME *is* making a difference', says Volmink. 'But we have to stop praying for miracles. We can't effect change with a quick approach and need to take a long-term view.'

To that end, CASME envisions itself expanding into the policy arena, perhaps developing effective pedagogical prototypes, while the state takes over the provision of educational programming. Volmink thus envisions CASME continuing to run with a small core staff which will implement model projects nationwide.

Creches Care
PO Box 32733
Glenstantia 0010
Phone: (012) 98-2041/2
Fax: (012) 998-9679

Don Macey of the Standard Bank Foundation loves Creches Care, a programme whose premise is simple and which applies the multiplier effect admirably. Yet it has not yet caught on in a big way in South Africa.

Creches Care, which started in 1987, is a two-pronged operation. The first prong consists of a programme targeting very poor black children in disadvantaged communities by offering an array of stimulation activities and school-readiness skills. The second targets unskilled child-minders in backyard creches who have almost no facilities to work with by offering them weekly courses to show them how they can improve their work and create learning materials with a minimum of money — and a lot of imagination.

The so-called "Accelerated Development Programme" which forms the structure of Creches Care curriculum was designed by executive director Mavis Pretorius and draws on university research which shows how early intervention can make a big difference in the learning ability of very young children from deprived areas.

Basically, the programme consists of five "mobile creches", buses converted into colourful play areas and equipped with a television, VCR, generator, and reading materials and appropriate toys. These units travel in five areas: Soweto, KaNgwane, Port Elizabeth (Kwanebuhle and Uitenhage), Botshabelo and Mangaung.

Each bus can accommodate 50 children, but has enough materials to serve another 50 playing outside, if necessary. It has a qualified pre-school teacher on board and, from Monday through Friday, makes three or four stops a day for two hours each. The bus visits each site once a week, so that up to 20 centres are reached in each area. While the teacher goes through a range of activities, the child-minder watches her work — and helps out, of course — and picks up valuable teaching skills in the process.

Each Friday morning from 8 am to 10 am, Creches Care sponsors adult education classes for child-minders and parents who are interested in more intensive training. These can include courses in basic toy-making, especially learning how to use "waste" products

Mrs Magdalen Dladla, Mother of the Year 1993, with the youth she is training, under the auspices of The Valley Trust, in activities which include painting and drama and music groups. These activities have been instrumental in keeping many children off the streets.

Kabelo Thalatse, Anna Nawa and Mmalefikana brushing up on their painting skills at the BMW Early Learning Centre.

A group of children who attend the Creches Care.

A Sunflower Projects trainee building team. Trainee builders from this project constructed a number of buildings at the Luthuli Centre.

Valley Trust programmes use labour-intensive strategies for public works.

Installing the ceilings at the Luthuli Centre.

A Valley Trust self-help housing project.

A Khuphuka Skills Training and Development Programme building project.

Hugh McLean of Liberty Life, and members of the Youth Development Programme.

Graduate of a Triple Trust leather-work training course.

Computer training at CRIC in the Western Cape.

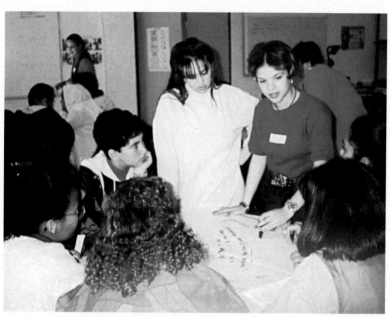

Students actively involved in a career choice workshop at CRIC.

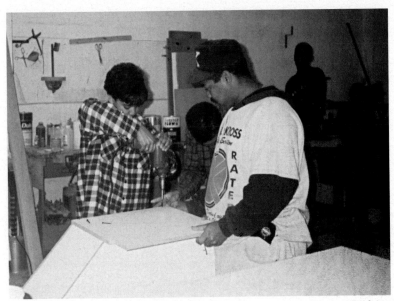

A CRIC work-experience programme – building kitchen units at AA Interiors. Bridging the gap between foundation and work.

Poultry farming at the Luthuli Centre.

Women installing irrigation pipes at the LIMA Centre, Umkomazi Valley.

An Eskom supported sewing school.

such as old tins and plastic containers to create musical instruments, dolls and other playthings.

Since most of these child-minders are untrained and provide mainly a care-taking service, the courses offer easy and very basic instruction in stimulation activities to encourage children to be more active and more verbal. They also have explicit aims in improving fine motor, cognitive and other skills, promoting better perceptual and emotional development, and providing preparation for a more structured school environment. On Friday afternoons the buses are cleaned.

The buses are driven by retired men who double as grandfather figures to the children and also sometimes assist with activities such as storytelling. 'They often take the children on their laps,' says Dina Terblanche, staff coordinator, who recalls seeing how one of the drivers picked up 'a little thingy that was crying' and calmed the child down.

Founder Mavis Pretorius, a trained social worker, and her late husband, Reverend Jan Pretorius, created Creches Care as a way to address the serious learning shortcomings in poor children who were not receiving any form of instruction in school-readiness skills and who were failing Grade One at a record rate. Drawing only on local funding, the project runs on a small scale but could be easily expanded with more funding.

The need is obvious. Many of the children have no access to professional child-minding or any real toys — or of a father figure in the home. The visiting buses give them only two hours of exposure per week, but these two hours are often the richest they get, and Creches Care research indicates that the benefits are real. 'One mother walked 15 kilometres once to meet with us and tell us how important the experience was, but especially mentioned how happy her child was when the driver picked him up,' says Dina Terblanche. 'There's no man in that household, and the mother said her child had been very happy with the experience.'

Key to the operation of Creches Care, Pretorius emphasises, is that the units are controlled by community representatives. Her office, consisting just of the two women, provides advisory services and raises funds to run the buses and the curriculum development.

**Eskom Community Development Programme & Corporate
Action Network**
c/o Eskom
PO Box 0191
Johannesburg 2000
Phone: (011) 800-2346
Fax: (011) 800-2340

One of the ways Eskom implements its CSI is to appoint community development officers who regularly spend time in the field to
liaise with small businesses and local community groups. They act
as a link with Eskom's electrification programme to help electrify
schools and other public amenities and to serve as a liaison with its
marketing department to encourage small business development
through electrification. Eskom participates in a Corporate Action
Network with several dozen other corporate members, who share
resources and information and sometimes cooperate on projects to
build small businesses.

I was taken on a day-long tour of several small Eskom-funded
projects to see how investment in electrification has made a difference. I accompanied members of a television production company
who were staking out possible locations for a documentary. Our
guide was Jenny Rogers, a community development officer in
Eskom's Johannesburg office. At each stop we were met by a
regional customer service representative who serves as a liaison
between Eskom and communities. The representatives — who were
all black — often come from the communities where they work, or
at least know them very well.

Our first stop was a squatter settlement in Doornkop, where substantial infrastructural development is under way, including the
construction of a new, full-service shopping centre. There we saw
three projects: a community creche that had been newly electrified,
so that the classroom as well as kitchen had electric lights, and the
kitchen also had a stove; a small butchery located in an old shipping
container which doubles as an electrical contractor's shop; and a
fast-food outlet run by a local minister where fish and chips can be
quickly fried.

The creche did not have a lot of equipment, but the children
appeared to be engaged in organised programmes rather than merely being cared for. The butchery was able to provide fresh meat to

a community where it would otherwise take a long trip — and taxi fare — to get it. The fast-food outlet provides extra income for the minister, who is investing some of it in building a new church nearby.

We also saw an Eskom customer service depot where community mail boxes have also been installed. These have solar lighting units that enable residents to pick up their mail safely at any time of day or night. The customer service depots are part of a network through which electricity users buy pre-paid cards which monitor electricity consumption through in-house meters which are connected to a central computer. The meters are marked with symbols (a happy face and a sad face) and lights to indicate when available electricity is almost used up.

We then went to Orange Farm, a rapidly growing area where we were shown a school under construction which Eskom is electrifying. In Vosloorus we visited a small shopping centre which houses several small business hives supported by the Small Business Development Corporation in which Eskom has been involved. In this case, Eskom has provided funding through the Corporate Action Network and assisted in electrifying the facility.

There are many dimensions to the work Eskom is doing. By electrifying communities, the company is creating new jobs for local electrical contractors and part-time vendors who can sell the meter cards from their homes if they want. And then, of course, other jobs are provided for butcheries and shops that want to sell fresh produce, cold beverages and other foodstuffs that require refrigeration. Other types of small businesses spin off from these primary businesses.

In addition, Eskom is increasingly joining partnerships with other companies so that projects can become more comprehensive even if the individual firms do not have large resources. So, for instance, it has joined with Gencor in a number of major school-building projects in which Gencor oversees the building and the training of local people to take part in it, while Eskom does the electrification.

Food Gardens Foundation
PO Box 41250
Craighall Park 2024
Phone: (011)880-5956
Fax: (011) 442-7642

On a sunny but windy day at the Ipelegeng Community Centre in Soweto, several dozen people are gathered for the ribbon-cutting ceremony of Soweto's new food gardens centre. Most of the people there have been through or are currently in a training programme run by the new Soweto branch of the Food Gardens Foundation (FGF), where they have learned basic skills in growing food gardens on small plots. Some have travelled here from the Northern Transvaal and the Free State to be honoured with certificates for completing the training.

The Gauteng Minister of Agriculture, John Mavuso, will cut the ribbon. He will also announce that the Ministry will donate land to FGF for future projects. It is a breakthrough for an organisation that was launched in 1977 with an annual budget of just R1 200. Nowadays, FGF has projects throughout Southern Africa, including projects targeting disabled people, schools and a wide range of community-based organisations. Its techniques have found their way as far north as Ghana, Uganda and Kenya.

Pauline Raphaely and Joy Niland founded what they called Food Gardens Unlimited as a way to promote basic self-help techniques in food growing to poor people with limited access to land, money and water, and who had minimal knowledge on how to get the most use out of what they did have. Initially targeting Soweto and Reef townships, the two women expanded their programme throughout the country.

Theirs is a bare-bones operation which, through extensive partnerships, enables them to keep their full-time staff to just 10. Many local corporate donors have helped out, including, in 1994, Gencor, Nedcor and the Southern Life Foundation.

FGF's programmes include the following:

1. a train-the-trainers programme to identify teachers, social workers and community activists to learn basic skills of growing food gardens and applying them to the communities in which they work;

2. lectures, demonstrations, workshops and video presentations

available in many languages to workers in health, education, community development and agriculture;
3. educational materials production, in the form of charts, comics, posters and other print materials;
4. follow-up visits from staff;
5. a low-cost seed service, plus guidelines on how to use them;
6. co-operation with existing organisations, such as schools, clinics, welfare organisations and government departments; and
7. networking with other development NGOs. For instance, READ compiled an educational resource package for teachers which includes information on food gardens and EcoLink developed a handbook on growing vegetable gardens.

It is a multi-disciplinary programme which, in addition to teaching about growing food also teaches about recycling (certain types of kitchen and veld rubbish can be turned into fertilizers), nutrition and the benefits of co-operative gardening through the formation of community gardens and food gardens clubs. It also has an income-generating component: surplus produce may be sold, providing gardeners with extra cash while they make fresh food available to their communities. FGF has extended its programmes into schools and has co-operated with the South African National Seed Organisation (SANSOR) and the Green Industries Council to promote the creation of Peace Gardens. SANSOR sponsors Peace Gardens competitions to honour community leaders who have formed peace gardens that have had an impact in their communities. Their names and projects are listed in the FGF 1993-94 executive report.

The Soweto Centre is a special case since it serves as a resource for the entire township. In addition to a model garden, it also has a nursery that sells seedings; a resource centre with information on seeds, plants and tools; a training centre; and a base for a full-time fieldworker. In addition, some of the funding FGF has received will be used as salaries for the two workers who have finished the trainee programme and are now maintaining the centre and providing training themselves.

FGF tries to avoid fostering a "dependency syndrome," so its trainees pay a basic fee for courses. It is nominal but an important part of their philosophy of promoting self-help and independence. New directions for FGF include an urban agriculture pilot project.

Get Ahead Foundation
PO Box 3776
Pretoria 0001
Phone: (012) 320-6530
Fax: (012) 320-8286

The offices of Get Ahead Foundation fill a two-storey Pretoria building, with loan officers and trainers busy helping new entrepreneurs and raising funds to keep projects going. But the real action is in townships and rural communities where the Foundation has provided loans along with entrepreneurship and technical training, and, more recently, loans for low-cost housing. It has become the prototype for successful micro-enterprise support, creating one new job for each R350 loan — and many spinoffs in the process.

I visited several Get Ahead projects in Mamelodi, joining a group of visiting executives from the Geneva offices of US chemical company Du Pont, a long-time Get Ahead funder. Our first stop was the home of welder Lukas Mokoena. His growing security gate business has prompted him to begin looking for a self-contained site. We saw several employees install a motorised gate at the home of a well-to-do local entrepreneur. Get Ahead has granted Lukas bridging finance to buy more equipment and hire assistants.

Our next stop was the backyard workshop of Daniel Molefo, who also welds security gates and builds window frames and braai stands. An assiduous worker who never takes a day off, he has sent his son and daughter to university to study medicine and law. After being retrenched from African Air, Molefo started his own business and turned to Get Ahead when he was unable to get bank loans elsewhere.

From having just one machine, Molefo used his R1 500 loan to buy additional tools and stock, and took free courses in business administration. Demand for his products has enabled him to hire assistants, thus creating further employment.

Further on, we visited the bustling Leseding Design School, whose founder, Frans Maluka, started a backyard sewing business in 1964 and now reports a turnover of more than R1 million a year, including 44 franchises in townships throughout South Africa. In the late 1980s, Maluka applied for a Get Ahead loan, but was turned down until he took courses in business management, bookkeeping and marketing, including advertising.

Advertising has made all the difference, says his daughter, Lilian, who runs the school these days: 'We're laughing all the way to the bank.' Maluka's school now occupies its own large building where courses are offered in basic and advanced sewing to women (and some men) from throughout the region. They pay R2 000 per year for their course and a further R40 per month to stay in an on-site hostel. These days, Maluka does the company's books, and his daughter is the MD.

Get Ahead was formed in 1984 by Archbishop Desmond Tutu, along with Soweto physician/businessman Dr Nthato Motlana, and other black business activists. From the outset, there was a political goal to Get Ahead's work: to empower black people in the informal sector, in the form of loans and training — there are no giveaways — without dependence on the state. Donations were solicited principally from foreign sources.

In recent years, however, Get Ahead has formed ties with provincial and state agencies and sought help from local firms. In 1993 the Durban City Council made R500 000 available for informal business lending through a Get Ahead initiative, and Get Ahead has linked up with the Independent Development Trust Finance Corporation for a new housing scheme. US Agency for International Development is a long-time supporter, and it announced a multi-million dollar loan in 1994.

Get Ahead's help generally takes the form of micro-loans, but also includes free training in such basic management skills as costing, pricing, marketing and bookkeeping, and technical skills (welding, panel beating, motor repairs, carpentry, sewing and knitting). It targets four types of clients: street hawkers; backyard manufacturers; business owners one step up from backyards, ie, rented spaces in business hives or other sites away from private homes; and self-contained, complete businesses.

To date, more than 20 000 borrowers have received loans from R200 to R2 000 (with an average of R450), and the Foundation estimates that it has created some 30 000 jobs in all, according to Wendy Richards. Get Ahead uses a group loan system, modelled after stokvels as well as the Grameen Bank in Bangladesh, the prototype for helping to make very poor people "bankable".

This revolving loan system assures that each member repays his or her loan on time. The interest rate is a relatively high 30 percent, but early repayments result in a discount, bringing the effective rate down to 22 percent.

The Foundation's new housing finance division helps blacks

buy a small site of land and materials to build a house or improve their current homes. Loans range from R2 000 to R20 000 and are often made through companies that have employee housing schemes. The programme follows strict criteria for borrowers (who must earn R2 000 or less), credit rating, proof of ownership of property, employment history, savings history (at least four months) and the capacity to enter into contracts. The loans last from one to three years.

Get Ahead has offices at 23 sites nationwide, mainly in townships in Gauteng, Natal, the Eastern Transvaal and the Cape. An office is being set up in the Free State.

Its Durban office reports making 808 loans in 1993; repayment rates were over 90 percent and delinquency levels were near zero. Its programme helped to create nearly 2 200 full-time jobs and about 1 900 part-time jobs. Nearly half of the loans went to support hawkers, about 20 percent each went to retailers and manufacturers, and 9 percent went to service jobs.

Joint Education Trust (JET)
PO Box 178
Wits 2050
Phone: (011) 339-3212/3, 339-3242/45
Fax: (011) 339-3246

The Joint Education Trust (JET) was established in 1991 as a five-year, R500 million programme to "kickstart" South Africa's ailing education system during the political transition. JET's mission is one of the most urgent and basic ones facing South Africa now: to promote the relationship between learning and the world of work by funding groups that provide a range of education and training to marginalised groups.

Key to JET's formation is the strategy of its funders — South Africa's largest corporate players. It arose from discussions between major corporations and the Urban Foundation to create a partnership that would link corporate donors with South Africa's leading education, labour, political and community organisations. They agreed to commit R500 million over five years, drawing this sum from outside their CSI budget, presumably to pre-empt the new government from imposing a reconstruction "tax" over which they would have no control.

In this way, the 14 corporate donors — AECI, Anglo American, Barlow Rand, Caltex, First National Bank, Gencor, JCI, Sankorp, Sanlam, Sasol, Shell, South African Breweries, Southern Life and Standard Bank — were able to call some of the shots; each company has the right to nominate a trustee to JET.

Meanwhile, to make JET balanced and legitimate, the companies sought out leading political, labour, black business and progressive educational groups to serve as partners. These included the ANC, Azapo, the IFP and the PAC; Cosatu, Nactu and the South African Democratic Teachers' Union; and the National Education Co-ordinating Committee and South Africa's two principal black business federations, Fabcos and Nafcoc. Each group also has the right to name a trustee.

In addition, JET has a full-time secretariat to run the organisation. Project officers and one project evaluation coordinator oversee the project selection process and the all-important follow-up to make sure that funds are being used appropriately. At this writing, JET was headed by acting director Dr Nick Taylor, formerly of the

Education Policy Unit of the University of the Witwatersrand, who took the reins from Professor N C Manganyi when he was named acting director-general of the Ministry of Education.

JET focuses on three areas for funding: (1) programmes that reach out to young people who missed out on quality education when they were of schoolgoing age (15 percent of funding in 1993); (2) teacher upgrading projects to improve the quality of teaching (51 percent in 1993); and (3) adult basic education programmes (34 percent in 1993). About 22 percent of JET's resources targets rural areas, one-third reaches rural and urban organisations, and 45 percent goes to urban centres. JET allocated R166 million for 176 projects in 1993.

Among the programmes profiled in this book, Albert Luthuli Community and Educational Development Trust (see Sunflower Project Profile on p179), Project Literacy, the TTO and The Valley Trust have received JET funding.

Khuphuka Skills Training and Employment Programme
3A Eaton Road
Congella 4001
Phone: (031) 255-530
Fax: (031) 259-320

The building that houses Khuphuka (Zulu for 'to move up') is an unassuming three-storey structure in a light industrial neighbourhood near Durban's central business district. The sign outside gives no indication of the activities inside.

Yet just beyond the very basic offices that house Khuphuka's management staff, a mini-RDP is under way. In a courtyard, two dozen men are practising bricklaying and masonry skills. Their "cement" is a soft temporary substance, and at the end of the day, they will dismantle all they have assembled, and learn new techniques tomorrow.

Upstairs, each room has a different construction activity under way, with "practice" and "real" projects taking place. A plumbing room has men learning how to install the plumbing for sinks, toilets and bathtubs. In the welding section, students are learning how to do basic welds, although some are doing more sophisticated projects, such as structural steelwork, security gates and hawkers' trolleys. In another section is an electricity workshop, where instruction is given on how to wire houses. Nearby, other Khuphuka trainees are wiring simple lamps and repairing kitchen appliances, including stoves.

On another floor is the woodshop. A large section has been allocated to build the woodframe for a model house; today the learners are being taught how to build roofs and install drain pipes. Nearby, young men — for just 5 percent of Khuphuka's trainees are women despite extensive efforts to recruit them — are sanding down the curved edges of desktops for new desks that have been commissioned by the University of Natal. The men are only in their second week, but the quality of the work, which is scrupulously supervised, is professional.

These activities, and more, at Khuphuka are breathtaking, but so, says director Stelios Comninos, is the deep degree of need; up to 65 percent of Durban's black workforce is unemployed. Since it opened its doors in late 1993, the programme has already put several hundred people from the community, including marginalised youth, ex-combatants, former political prisoners and returnees through its training programme.

As much as possible, the trainees are associated with established community trusts, so that they will have projects to return to when they complete the course. They are enrolled generally as a group rather than individually, and they are required to pay a "commitment fee" of R25 per week. In addition, Khuphuka operates a fully-fledged construction company, Zizamele Development Systems (ZDS), which does building production.

Trainees at Khuphuka receive instruction in modules for three to 13 weeks and then join an on-site practical training programme in their communities in which they receive a basic training allowance which increases as their skills improve. Many projects are linked with community or commercial contracts, so that participants know there are customers for their products.

ZDS has already been involved with building a number of classrooms and clinics in Umlazi and The Valley Trust as well as a community centre at Mpola. In addition, in view of the shortage of jobs in the formal sector, Khuphuka encourages self-employment by offering courses in topics such as budgeting and banking in order to encourage some trainees to set up their own informal businesses.

Comninos spent many years in exile in Zimbabwe, where he helped develop a successful training programme which has served as a prototype for Khuphuka. Here, he is among 52 administrators and trainers, of whom just five are white; there has been a real effort at affirmative action in the way this tightly-run programme is structured.

Khuphuka received initial funding from various European donors. At this writing, the only South African corporate funder was the Liberty Life Foundation, which, Comninos says, committed R100 000 when the project was still getting off the ground — an unusual move for a corporate funder.

Lima Rural Development Foundation
PO Box 93
Umzumbe 4225
Phone & Fax: (0391) 846-262/846-102

Turn right from the Umzumbe exit going south on the ocean front N2 highway from Durban, and after following a few basic directions, you will find yourself on a bumpy dirt road far from the affluent beach resort communities that you passed on your left. On a hilltop is an old farm which now serves as the offices for LIMA, an agricultural development NGO based in southern KwaZulu.

LIMA — the Zulu word for "plough" — is a rural development project run by Duncan Stewart, an agriculturalist who worked for the Kwazulu government for 10 years and wanted to get involved with an organisation that allowed him more flexibility and creative opportunity. After exploring the possibility of working with other organisations or NGOs, he decided to start his own — and on his own.

Founded in 1989, LIMA currently operates in three areas of Natal, where its activities include irrigation schemes, forestry development, labour-intensive road-building and extension support to small farmers to improve their agricultural techniques and their business and marketing skills. Most participants in these projects are women. And while the head office has just a handful of administrative staff, most of LIMA's 40-odd employees are in the field, providing engineering, economic and agricultural assistance.

Over time, LIMA has branched out into other types of projects, including a food gardens project (funded by the Independent Development Trust, with 600 women taking part), labour-based dam construction and general capacity-building. For example, LIMA is helping with what Stewart calls the "village-isation" of rural areas that have become more densely populated, by promoting road-building and water-supply projects and helping with the establishment of new municipal structures to provide community services.

The ultimate aim of whatever LIMA does is to empower communities to become self-sufficient. In the Bergville region of the Drakensberg, an area Stewart describes as a conservative black and white area, LIMA set up the Ulwazi Business Advice and Community Centre in order to provide resource information on careers and community planning. Ulwazi has been spun off from Lima and is an autonomous Section 21 company, and Stewart serves as a consultant.

In the same region, LIMA has begun a project to explore land rentals within tribal areas. The project is being run in conjunction with the University of Natal and is funded by the Development Bank of Southern Africa.

A distinctive feature about LIMA is its philosophy of development. 'We take a commercial, more conventional approach. We're entrepreneurial,' says Stewart, who notes that the fertilisers that LIMA sells to farmers at cost in its programme are commercial products that contain chemicals. This is in contrast to other organisations, which run some similar types of programmes, but emphasise organic techniques. 'Those approaches are not practical for the type of work we do,' affirms Stewart.

In addition, LIMA now generates most of its operating income from consulting and subcontracts. For example, its "Project Grow" draws on contracts with Sappi Forests in which 1 600 small farmers within southern KwaZulu have set up small commercial woodlands. And although LIMA had no ties with KwaZulu departments when it was started, it now has a number of contracts with them. (Stewart emphasises LIMA's apolitical stance and notes that he has always worked closely with tribal authorities because not doing so would undermine some projects.)

In addition, LIMA worked on a one-off project with the National Union of Mineworkers to set up irrigation schemes and community gardens to enable retrenched mineworkers to launch agricultural cooperatives.

LIMA solicits corporate support and other sponsorships (such as the German Embassy funding) for specific capital projects or one-off capital items, such as tractors and farm implements, and is therefore not donor-dependent. Only a few corporate donors are listed in its 1992-93 annual report, and the largest grant from these is R30 000 (from South African Breweries) which is modest compared to the huge grants The Valley Trust receives. Others include Anglo American, Anglovaal, National Beverage Services (now Coca-Cola South Africa), Premier Group and 3M Company.

LIMA's 1994-95 budget was R2,2 million, up from R700 000 two years earlier. Stewart estimates that LIMA's labour-based projects currently employ about 2 200 people in relatively constant work, engage 2 000 forestry farmers (of whom 70 percent are women), reach about 7 500 families through its water supply projects, and directly assist about 200 irrigation farmers (60 percent women). Since most households have eight to 10 people, many more benefit.

Stewart, who was raised on a farm in Natal and spoke Zulu as his first language, knows his constituency well. Taking a visitor on a tour of projects through the Umzumbe River valley, he was continually greeted, and gave lifts in his bakkie to several men on our visit, including a local headman. This type of community intimacy is essential to being able to define a clear project vision, but LIMA's professional approach, including its astute balance between contracts and donations, plus its transparency, explain its rapid growth and strong reputation.

Project Literacy (PROLIT)
PO Box 57280
Arcadia 0007
Phone: (012) 323-3447/4543/4595
Fax: (012) 324-3800

In the minimum security prison at Leeuwkop, two classrooms are filled with young men who are studying basic English. One class is a bit more advanced than the other, but in neither case as yet are the students much beyond the primary school level. Their teachers provide gentle prodding to get them through their work and prison personnel make sure things are going smoothly without being too intrusive.

The students are on display today: the SABC has come to interview and videotape them for a possible news story, and Nedcor's Hilary Ashton has come to announce its donation to the project. (Anglo American, JCI and Liberty Life have also made donations.) On the lawn outside the classroom, tables have been set up with *hors d'oeuvres* and beverages for the visiting media and prison officials. No information is given about how the men landed up here; what is important — and represents a breakthrough for the institution — is that Project Literacy (PROLIT), which runs this programme, has been allowed to happen in the first place and that prison officials support this initiative. When the men leave, they'll have been given the opportunity to learn new skills that will help them find employment or at least enable them to continue their schooling to a more advanced level.

If this project succeeds, illiterate young men will have reached Standard Five equivalency in just two years. It is a huge gamble, but if it works, this experiment could have enormous impact on new national planning programmes for adults who deserve a second chance at learning. Some probably never had much of first chance to begin with.

The pilot literacy project at Leeuwkop is one of many programmes run by PROLIT, an NGO founded in 1973 in Pretoria as a grassroots voluntary effort that operated from church buildings and defied the Group Areas Act. In 1986 PROLIT launched a trust fund to provide an endowment for growth. And now it is a sophisticated national operation with a large full-time staff working out of a newly renovated three-storey building in Pretoria that PROLIT now owns.

The pattern of PROLIT's "coming of age" is similar to that of a number of NGOs that struggled during the apartheid era to provide needed services that the government was not interested in offering and is now courting the current government for support. It often services other NGOs in setting up projects. In addition to corporate backing, it has received funding from JET.

PROLIT's focus is adult learners, many of whom had little or no education, and work — if indeed they are employed — in very low-wage jobs. Its four areas of work include curriculum development, adult education centres, training and upgrading for teachers of adult learners, and a basic education extension programme for companies and community groups that want to run their own adult basic education projects.

PROLIT is placing special attention on rural areas and is also experimenting with computer-aided learning. It has high-impact potential. While its adult education centres reach more than 2 000 learners each year, its teacher training programme makes it possible to reach even more: each trained literacy teacher can work with at least 20 learners each year on a part-time basis and at least 60 if teaching full time.

So the organisation's new emphasis on teacher training offers great promise to reach many more people.

READ Educational Trust
PO Box 30994
Braamfontein 2017
Phone: (011) 339-5941/0
Fax: (011) 403-2311

Michael O'Dowd of the Anglo American and De Beers Chairman's Fund takes pride in boasting of the company's role in 1979 in helping to launch one of South Africa's "real success stories": the READ Educational Trust, an organisation which creates libraries in poor communities throughout South Africa. READ, whose board of trustees O'Dowd now chairs, is one of South Africa's best-known and most mainstream NGOs.

READ — which stands for Read Educate And Develop — arose in the post-1976 era to address the demands for better libraries and reading facilities in black townships. Founder and national director Cynthia Hugo describes it as a direct response to the State President's directive to the private sector to take on the challenge since the state couldn't (or wouldn't).

Hugo, then a librarian at St John's College, and a colleague, who were already involved in literacy work in Soweto, recruited other private school librarians to run a book-collecting project. But, says Hugo, they didn't want leftovers: 'We felt these should be the right books at the right time — they needed to be attractive books that would motivate children.' They linked up with a literacy committee in Soweto made up of students, community and women's groups and other organisations that sought to supply libraries in the township's 50 high schools.

A pivotal event in READ's development was a luncheon for the parents of children from St John's and other private schools. Many parents were executives at South Africa's top companies, and the organisers put on a display of books — donated for this purpose — that could be bought for R3 000. By meal's end, Hugo and her colleagues had raised R150 000 in start-up funds for READ; Anglo American pledged the first grant to cover staff salaries.

'It's motherhood and apple pie,' says Hugo, explaining READ's widespread corporate, embassy and foundation support. But this doesn't mean funding is constant or consistent. She is troubled by the policy of some donors to limit grants to short periods and require new applications every year or two or status reports as often as twice a year. 'Development is a long process,' she insists. 'You often don't see results for at least three years.' Besides, she notes, READ has a long track record and a policy of total transparency.

No longer just a supplier of libraries, READ now has 93 full-time staff, operates 11 regional centres in South Africa (and one in Namibia), has funded over 1 800 educational institutions, is expanding into adult literacy and has trained an estimated 50 000 people at colleges and community centres people since its inception. Its materials include specialised "skills packs" in such areas as geography and science as well as story packs; and it develops videotapes and wall charts to promote learning and language instruction.

Key to READ's work is keeping current on new developments in literacy and their application to daily life. As its directors see it, READ doesn't just teach reading; it also promotes creative and logical thinking, problem-solving, a broader understanding of world events and better working relations between teachers, parents and children.

READ's 1993 budget was nearly R11 million. More than 90 percent covered programming while the balance went for training, development and administration. The organisation has been so successful in fundraising that it reported a surplus at year-end 1993 which was transferred into a "stabilisation" fund for future projects. This is not always the case for READ, which must constantly raise new funds for materials development and distribution as well as training.

Increasingly, READ is aiding literacy programmes in the workplace, from instruction in basic mother tongue literacy and beginner English to courses in conversational English, vocational English and advanced English. READ trains trainers within a company to teach literacy, provides materials and offers a monitoring and follow-up service to ensure that the programme runs as planned.

READ also helps companies develop self-study programmes and study skills (such as note-taking, reading effectively and using a library), to create in-house libraries and design company-funded community libraries.

Through shrewd cause-related marketing arrangements, READ musters corporate support while the sponsor promotes its products. A READ programme is advertised on Kellogg's cereal boxes, while other company logos are printed on teaching aids. First National Bank has full-page ads in READ's 1993 and 1994 annual reviews, and other firms lend *pro bono* support for advertising, human resources, legal advice and other services.

A new trend at READ — as at other NGOs — is to form partnerships with other development organisations, government and the communities in which it works. 'You must be very flexible,' says Hugo. 'In many communities we workshop our projects with local stakeholders to find out what *they* want before we come in.'

Furthermore, READ is trying, when possible, to produce materials locally. Its *Big Books* are the first of its products to be printed in South Africa; others had been imported at great expense. The *Big Books* encourage the use of languages other than English.

Sunflower Projects
PO Box 26250
Isipingo Beach 4115
Phone: (031) 902-5856
Fax: (031) 902-7757

Driving north from Durban toward Groutville on Natal's North Coast, Jonathan Smith, Project Development Manager of Sunflower Projects, describes the buildings he's going to show me. We'll be visiting the Albert Luthuli Centre for Education and Development, a new service organisation which provides a range of educational, training, job creation and recreation programmes to a community of 70 000 divided by politics, conflicts between Mozambican refugees and local residents, and disputes over land ownership and land use (pitting cane growers against cattle farmers).

Sunflower trainees built its head office building as well as two long, one-storey buildings with workspace for spaza shops, tailors, a panel beater, the local health committee, a hair salon and other small businesses and organisations serving a poor community that is growing fast as squatters head its way. They also built a two-storey community hall that has a large stage along with meeting rooms for community groups. A few days from now, Nelson Mandela is going to be here to formally launch the Centre, and preparations are under way for this event.

While Murray & Roberts is the principal funder of Sunflower, other organisations have pitched in to make the Luthuli Centre possible, including the Joint Services Board, which financed the capital cost of the structures; the Department of Manpower, which funded the building skills training programmes; Kagiso Trust, which "kick-started" it with a R400 000 grant; the Small Business Development Corporation, which installed containers for shops; Eskom, which donated transformers to electrify the Centre; and the Hexagon Trust, which sponsors upgrading courses for science teachers.

Murray & Roberts launched Sunflower Projects in 1985 as a for-profit training initiative that would derive most of its income from the Department of Manpower. Under contract from Manpower, it aimed to train unemployed men and women in the building and related trades, and also offer classes in literacy and numeracy, with a focus on basic bookkeeping, accounting and costing, so that they might set up their own small businesses.

But the approach resulted in a somewhat hybrid CSI: it was not purely CSI because of its profit motive, even though all profits were to be ploughed into the Murray & Roberts Foundation. But nor was it run according to strict business terms because of the nature of its programme.

'It was a blurred vision,' admits Smith of Sunflower's Durban office. 'There was an inherent conflict between the time pressure to produce and the need to allow for training.' This conflict, plus a cut in Manpower Department support, almost forced Sunflower to close down a few years ago. Murray & Roberts reorganised it and absorbed its losses, and at the end of 1993, after retrenching nearly half of its 50-member staff, a leaner but stronger-rooted Sunflower emerged as a not-for-gain Section 21 company that solicits outside funding and generates income from contracts.

In addition, rather than focus on training people with no skills who would probably be unemployed once a project is finished, Sunflower now seeks to identify black contractors to run some of its projects and helps them employ and train local workers. This process upgrades the credentials of the contractors, who are able to get professional certification, and continues to provide training and short-term employment for people who lack skills.

And by going "back to doing what we do best" — construction-related activities and not literacy and other forms of training that other NGOs are better equipped to provide — Smith believes the new Sunflower Projects is much better positioned to carry out RDP-related training to build housing and community projects.

Projects on the drawing board include a 'Peace Initiative Project' in Wembezi township near Estcourt, in which local black contractors, under the supervision of Sunflower, will restore schools damaged in violence and two former National Economic Forum-funded projects: one on Natal's South Coast to build creches and community halls and the other in Mpophomeni, near Howick, to build industrial hives and a small training centre.

In addition to seeking out black contractors to head up its work, Sunflower is collaborating with the Development Management Trust (DMT) to assist in the "pre-contract" process to map out how and where a project will be built. This is a time-intensive process for which Sunflower is not paid, but the DMT exists to help with the consultative process and is funded for it. (Finding trainees is never a problem; they come to Sunflower, says Smith.)

Sunflower is not quite "out of the woods" during the difficult transition to a Section 21 company. For while it is trying to muster contracts that will cover its budget, it still needs outside funding support, and the Murray & Roberts Foundation refuses to be the sole funder. But Smith is optimistic that the restructured Sunflower Projects will get back on track; it is the right project at the right time.

The Toybox Project
c/o Human Sciences Research Council
Private Bag X41
Pretoria 0001
Phone: (012) 202-2587
Fax: (012) 2511

The Toybox project, better known as the "Coke Toybox", was devised as a way to provide "appropriate" toys for children in both urban and rural areas who lack access to real toys. But playing is just one function of these toys; they also aim to help develop children's cognitive and motor skills.

The concept was developed by Christine Liddell, a psychologist formerly at the Human Sciences Research Council, and the project was launched in 1988 with a R500 000 grant from Coca-Cola South Africa. Its current project coordinator is HSRC senior researcher Jennifer Kemp.

The toybox is the size of a large trunk and contains 56 items for use by about 50 children at a given time. These include toddler toys, puzzles with large and small pieces, workbooks, colouring books, crayons, a wheelbarrow, fabric dolls, pegboards, a number sorter, a shape sorter, number blocks and a set of wooden blocks, wooden cars, balls, a series of "conversation" posters, a weather chart, a body poster, skipping ropes, rubber quoits and a trolley block system.

They are made of durable materials and are designed to last; the toybox is evaluated regularly and toys are replaced every two years. Some 1 700 of the boxes have been assembled and distributed, reaching an estimated 62 000 children.

As the funder, Coke embeds brand consciousness among the young toy users at an early age: several large sacks containing blocks and toys are emblazoned with the red and white Coca-Cola logo. Some 1 700 boxes have been produced to date and most have been distributed to children's centres. All toyboxes are donated, which is essential for the organisations that receive them, since each one costs more than R2 000, which works out at about R40 per child, a very cost-effective programme.

And the toyboxes work: I saw one in use at the pre-school section of the Bophelo Community School (see Bophelo-Impilo Profile on p151), where little boys ran around with a toddle toy that consists of a steering wheel on a pole with a single wheel at its end, and the colourful story charts were on prominent display in the classrooms.

And at a creche in a squatter settlement in Doornkop, which Eskom electrified, an otherwise toyless facility had obtained a Coke Toybox, although it was in storage when I visited. (Kemp says HSRC warns recipients that if they do not allow children to use the toys, the toybox will be removed and given to child-minders who will use them.)

Testing has already shown that the toyboxes yield results. First of all, they're not just given out for random play; child-minders are trained in how to use them, especially for school-readiness skills. An HSRC study, which compared 200 children who had been exposed to the toybox with another 200 who hadn't but who were in the same age range, gender and came from similar socio-economic backgrounds, demonstrated better performance in all 12 areas being measured, in seven of which the Toybox users performed significantly better.

An interesting change in the toybox development process is a switch to manufacturing toys locally rather than obtaining them from Europe and North America. The HSRC found that some of the imported toys were irrelevant to rural South African children who could not recognise images in puzzles and charts that included zoo animals, steam trains and circus clowns.

One study showed that children were so confused by a puzzle made up of images they didn't know that they tried putting them in upside down. These were replaced with rural scenes that included farm animals and landscapes familiar to the children. Such adaptation is part of an ongoing process to make the toybox a much more meaningful, and more South African, product.

Foundations for a New Democracy

Toyota Teach
Primary School Project
PO Box 72632
Mobeni 4060
Phone: (031) 902-6596/9312
Fax: (031)902-4168

Piet Visagie takes a measured sigh when he describes Toyota Teach, which takes a unique approach to science and maths education. Recruited out of retirement in 1991 to coordinate the five-year, R8 million pilot programme, the former school principal from Pietermaritzburg now keeps a more hectic schedule than ever — and loves it. 'This is the most productive phase of my life,' he says.

For one thing, he has a hands-on role in an exciting new project. For another, there's a unique freedom from the red tape, internal politics and shortage of funds that marked his previous job. At Toyota Teach, the money isn't a problem, and Visagie has had a minimum of hassle with internal school politics. And members of the six NGOs that have developed and run the project get along, he says.

The Toyota South Africa Foundation established Toyota Teach following a survey it commissioned of primary schools in the Umlazi and Umbumbulu regions, where many Toyota employees live. The survey which revealed serious problems in the teaching of maths and science, and identified four root causes: poor school management; inadequate teaching of English which made studies in these areas difficult; a lack of qualified teachers in these subjects, and an overdependence on rote learning.

The decision to focus on primary schools was taken in part because programmes such as CASME (see the CASME Profile on p155), which works with secondary school teachers, already had considerable corporate support.

To maximise its impact, Toyota Teach, like CASME, targets teachers rather than going directly into the classroom. It works with teachers at 36 primary schools which feed students into three high schools that Toyota already supports, directly involving 1 080 teachers and indirectly reaching 45 000 students.

The Toyota South Africa Foundation recruited Visagie to coordinate the programme, and identified six NGOs to develop and run it. These include the READ Educational Trust, which encourages reading and builds libraries; the Centre for Cognitive

184

Development, which works to empower teachers and school principals; the Primary Science Project, an Urban Foundation spin-off; the Natal College of Education; and two programmes run by Radmaste (which stands for Research and Development in Mathematics, Science and Technology Education), based at University of the Witwatersrand, one in primary mathematics and the other in teacher accreditation.

In a collaboration rare for NGOs, these six have found a way to work together, drawing on their individual strengths.

The actual programme consists of several parts: 1) workshops and seminars to increase teaching competence, help change the negative perceptions among pupils towards maths and science and raise teachers' self-esteem about their work; 2) the development of more and better textbooks and equipment; 3) advocacy of policy changes within schools to increase teacher and principal involvement; and 4) cooperation with the KwaZulu education ministry.

Toyota-owned premises near Durban provide lecture rooms and offices for the programme. For 1996, when the pilot phase is over, Visagie said Toyota hopes to get steady funding from its Japanese parent to maintain and expand the programme.

The results of Toyota Teach training are encouraging so far. Two visitors from Japan who compared Toyota Teach schools with non-participating schools noticed key differences. Teachers use more illustrations and other classroom aids, and, more importantly, they 'ask more questions', says Visagie. And there is no such thing as "right" or "wrong" answers; children are learning to think about different possibilities. It's a huge change from the rote learning which has been endemic to black schools and particularly problematic in the teaching of science and maths.

As for the participating NGOs, they meet together eight times a year to coordinate their progress, while a steering committee chaired by the Toyota South Africa Foundation's Archie Nkabinde meets four times a year to assess progress, address problems and examine how to change the programme if necessary. An Action Committee meets as the need arises to address urgent issues. Visagie himself makes regular visits to the schools, distributing new maths pages to teachers and sometimes working with the principals. Some of the changes since the programme got into its stride include:

- making sure that school principals participate in, or at least are aware of, Toyota Teach from the outset. A few who were excluded have been somewhat obstructive to the programme, Visagie notes;

- second, teachers are now included in the assessment and evaluation teams along with the NGOs, which initially worked on their own. This has been a very important change and gives teachers a greater sense of "ownership" of the programme;
- and third, parents are made aware of the existence of the programme, as a way to encourage them to enthuse their children. This is sometimes a difficult process, Visagie explains, since not all parents take the same approach to learning; some are professionals but others are illiterate. With time, Toyota Teach hopes to plant the seeds to train students who are better skilled for professional training.

Triple Trust Organisation (TTO)
PO Box 13227
Mowbray 7705
Phone: (021) 448-7341
Fax: (021) 448-7321

In some ways, the Triple Trust Organisation (TTO) comes across as slick. Its pamphlets, donor newsletters and annual reports look professional in their clean design on black and white recycled paper, while its product brochures are printed in colour on glossy paper.

By using quality design and paper, by reaching out to donors, and by being utterly transparent, TTO is saying that an NGO doesn't have to "look" poor, constantly struggle or hold back information needed to do the type of work it does and to do it well. TTO provides wide-ranging support for emerging enterprises, with an emphasis on promoting self-employment among disadvantaged communities in the Cape peninsula.

Taking a business-like approach, TTO meets many urgent needs, offering skills and basic business training; granting mini-loans for start-up capital equipment; developing markets for the products clients make; providing business mentoring for emerging entrepreneurs; and matching new producers with volunteer business consultants from the corporate sector.

TTO also serves other NGOs, formal business and micro-enterprises, who draw on TTO's expertise and track record. This is done through an arm called Triple Trust Consulting, which was formed as an official division of TTO in 1993. Triple Trust Consulting helps NGOs write fundraising proposals, manage their funding portfolios, train staff to provide legal advice, and help link formal businesses to entrepreneurs in the informal sector.

TTO was launched in 1988 by James Thomas, a manpower trainer who had received exemption from military service on religious grounds and was seconded to the Department of Manpower in Cape Town as an inspector in its Unemployed Training Programme. Thomas felt that the training offered by Manpower was inadequate to help new businesses get going, so when his stint there ended, he started a small training consultancy, which became the seed for TTO. (The "Triple" refers to the assistance required for new micro-enterprises to succeed, in terms of training, financing and marketing.)

One of the first funders Thomas approached was the Southern Life Foundation, which agreed to help at the outset; the Foundation's Virginia Ogilvie Thompson, who serves on TTO's board, recalls being extremely impressed by the clear vision reflected in goals listed in Thomas's business plan.

These goals included maintaining a sense of community ownership of projects and courses; developing training courses in skills which would require low start-up costs for the potential entrepreneur and which would enable the entrepreneur to earn a living wage; supporting businesses with low start-up costs so as to avoid high debt build-up; using appropriate technology; teaching skills that have several applications; promoting self-employment; developing products for which there are real markets; ensuring easy access to raw materials and markets; and training people in skills for which there is a real demand.

TTO's courses include eight-week training programmes in sewing, leatherwork, knitting and butchery, and two-week "trader training" programmes in practical selling techniques and developing the motivation to sell. Courses are currently taught at 20 training centres in disadvantaged communities through the Western Cape, usually in facilities such as churches and community centres which invite TTO in. About 1 000 people are trained by TTO each year.

TTO's structure consists of four non-profit associations: the Neighbourhood Training Trust, the Self-Help Financing Trust, the Africa Trading Co-operative Trust and the Triple Trust Organisation. Each has a separate fund-raising number. (Donations to the Neighbourhood Training Trust are completely tax-deductible as a concession to educational and training institutions.) TTO has a full-time staff of 70.

Targeting overseas as well as local markets, TTO's trading arm has developed such products as keyrings and hairclips, small purses and large handbags; earrings and belts and sheepskin slippers in childrens' and adult sizes that would appeal to overseas buyers.

I visited TTO's offices, where I obtained some of the material and saw product samples as well as "The BEST Game" (which stands for Business Expenses Savings Training, a business training game which uses simulation role-playing to introduce aspiring entrepreneurs to basic business principles in simulated situations. I'd wanted to buy one, thinking it would cost no more than R100, but the price was R1 475.) Southern helped to fund the development of the game as well as a handbook, *Idea to Enterprise*, which describes the TTO technique to identify, evaluate and launch an idea to create informal sector employment.

TTO could almost be called a "state of the art" NGO, which appears to be doing almost everything right. In addition to receiving support from many South African corporate funders, it has enjoyed backing from a number of embassies and foreign donors as well as the Independent Development Trust and the JET.

In a booklet describing TTO's background, Thomas expresses his hope of convincing South Africa's new government to support TTO and similar projects which can be economically replicated nationwide. The TTO's 1993 annual report carries endorsements from Nelson Mandela and Archbishop Desmond Tutu.

The Valley Trust
PO Box 33
Bothas Hill 3660
Phone: (031) 777-1930
Fax: (031) 777-1114

The Valley Trust in Natal has been a model for Southern African NGOs. For one thing, its approach to service delivery requires aid recipients to take responsibility in policy-making and programmes. For another, it maintains total transparency and accountability to its donors. Third, its holistic approach to development integrates health (including nutrition and sanitation), education, job training and infrastructure (housing and clinics). And, finally, it works: the Trust's track record spans more than four decades.

'Marketing and fundraising have always been one of our strengths,' says Executive Director Keith Wimble, who has a background in medicine and business. 'We make regular report-backs, we meet our deadlines and we welcome audits of donations.'

There's also an ethos of democracy in the Trust's giving policy. While big funders are aggressively sought out (the Trust's projected 1993-94 budget was R14,6 million), small donors are welcome. The Trust's annual report lists all individual and institutional contributors, known as members, from those who gave as little as R10 to those whose grants reach the high six-figures.

From its founding in 1951, when Dr Halley Stott built a primary health care clinic in Bothas Hill, 30 minutes from Durban, the Trust aimed to promote community empowerment through self-help projects that link health with nutrition, agriculture, soil and water conservation, and appropriate technology.

Nowadays, 90 full-time staff members — including quite a few who have been there many years, an anomaly among NGOs where rapid turnover is the norm — oversee projects throughout the region, home to 100 000 people in five tribal groups. These include mobile health and training units as well as a modern medical clinic.

But nothing is given away for free. Besides having project input through democratically elected development committees, residents must contribute 10 percent of the value of any new facility, either through "sweat equity" or funds. A basic clinic visit costs R9 while a 25-litre container of water costs seven cents.

Agriculture has always been key to the Trust's programming,

and its eco-agriculture unit provides environmental education through demonstration gardens. Sixty-four vegetable gardens dot the valley, and the Trust runs a four-acre food yard and a social forestry unit to promote tree planting.

The education unit has 44 pre-schools; two education resources projects, which include a computer centre and offer teaching and school management skills to professional staff; and adult education in general or workplace literacy and numeracy as well as health and nutrition.

An exchange programme between local schools and St Mary's in Kloof enables children from the valley to learn English and participate in other activities; local teachers meet with St Mary's teachers to exchange ideas on teaching methods.

The Trust co-operates with major funders and NGOs. The Urban Foundation obtained funding for the Trust for 160 class-rooms, and the Independent Development Trust pledged to fund the construction of 'VIPs' — Ventilated Improved Pit latrines. Durban-based Sunflower Projects (see Sunflower Projects Profile on p179) assisted in renovating the Trust's education offices. Other joint projects have been run with the READ Educational Trust, the Rural Foundation, Operation Hunger and Habitat for Humanity, an American NGO.

Trust operations have been substantially streamlined and professionalised in recent years: Keith Wimble's job replaced that of a group manager and a medical consultant, and he consolidated 12 operating sections into 9. The Trust's volunteer programme follows strict criteria: volunteers may stay for no less than three months and no longer than one year.

Some learn techniques that they bring back to their home communities; others bring skills. An Israeli woman from a kibbutz introduced intercropping into the Trust's demonstration gardens, spreading legumes under maize plants. This process fixed nutrients into the land and improved land use efficiency. She cultivated culinary herbs as the underlayer and retailed them in Durban shops, but also used intercropping to develop medicinal herbs for local use by traditional healers.

Like many large NGOs, The Valley Trust is seeking to become financially self-sufficient and to replicate its programmes elsewhere. Its long-term strategy is to create an endowment that will generate enough income to cover programme costs. At that point, fundraising would target new programmes and capital projects, such as a maternity clinic, or assist programmes elsewhere.

Some cooperation is already under way. With funding from the Nedcor Community Development Trust, The Valley Trust recently helped manage a nutrition project in Vosloorus township in the Vaal, using untouched packaged airline food. This project also created jobs for local people and promoted nutrition education.

Youth Development Programme (YDP)
PO Box 10499
Johannesburg 2000
(for information contact The Liberty Life Foundation
Phone: (011) 408-3298
Fax: (011) 408-3998)

Phillip, a young man of 24, asked me two questions the day I came to visit: Where did I come from and how I could help his group? Along with about 14 other Soweto youths between the ages of 19 and 24, he has been involved in a self-upliftment project that was formed in 1992, one year after he and some fellow students failed their matric; their initial goal was to create a study group to prepare to rewrite the exam and pass it, and they're now doing much more to improve themselves. One thing Phillip knows for sure is that the only way to get extra help is to ask for it.

Quite a number of group members *did* pass — nine since the group got together — but they decided to stay together, both to acquire skills for themselves and then, Phillip explains, 'to teach skills to other people'. And with help from Liberty Life Foundation, the Youth Development Programme (YDP) has undertaken a number of projects to do just that.

As with some larger funded projects, YDP did not just "luck out" in finding a friend at Liberty Life; connections made the difference (as they did when librarian Cynthia Hugo sought funding for a township book distribution project which became the READ Educational Trust).

Another YDP member, Andrew, had known Hugh McLean in Bophuthatswana in the early 1980s when McLean was teaching there, and they had kept in touch. When Phillip, Andrew and the others began organising the group, they approached McLean for advice and support — and got both.

What makes YDP interesting is its replicability and the assistance that the Liberty Life Foundation provides. It represents a model "adopt-a-project", and the multiplier potential is great. But it takes a close relationship with and understanding of the young people involved, substantial inputs of time, and lots of patience.

Results are not instant. But the students don't expect that; at a time when there are no jobs, they are merely 'struggling for a normal life, and we have lots of joy working together', says Jubilee, another YDP member.

YDP does not have an office, but members meet daily, have taken courses together in basic computer skills, and, more important, says McLean, they have continued improving themselves through a structure and discipline that keeps them going and gives them hope at a frustrating time in their lives.

YDP has a constitution, elected officers to uphold it, and a disciplinary committee which penalises or expels members who are consistently late or absent for inappropriate reasons. The group has avoided seeking publicity because 'we're not ready yet', says Phillip.

YDP has had a number of unexpected dividends. Its founders, who were exceptionally motivated to begin with, have become more confident, determined and resourceful. For example, they have run AIDS education programmes at local schools and sponsored voter education at community centres. In addition, they have learned to run a budget and gained other management skills.

At one point, several of them got together to apply for clerical jobs at a bank. This process required discussions of how to prepare for a job interview, including how to develop a resume and how to present oneself. Another member approached several companies, unsuccessfully, about getting part-time jobs. McLean, who visits YDP regularly and lets its young leaders use the Foundation's copying machines and telephones, especially likes the way that development has been linked to broader needs.

As for the long term, YDP is exploring the possibility of developing a community centre in Soweto that they want to design and run. This idea is still in a preliminary stage, but Phillip and the others are confident that they can pull it off — with some help. 'There are no youth as organised as we are,' he claims. 'We've been marginalised for so long and now we want to prove that youth can do things on their own.'

PART III

Beyond CSI

CHAPTER 7

Socially responsible investing: The other side of social investment

Socially responsible investing (SRI) can be called the "flip side" of CSI. While companies create a CSI budget to provide direct support to community projects, SRI is a way for them, and other individual and institutional investors, to invest for financial return with a social dividend.

This section provides an overview of SRI in South Africa as an additional means to support South Africa's redevelopment. It includes a brief history of SRI worldwide, a review of its current status, a discussion of SRI in South Africa and an examination of other forms of social investing.

Background of SRI
SRI began in the US in the 1920s, when church groups protested investments in so-called "sin stocks" in liquor and tobacco products, or in companies involved with gambling. But it wasn't until the late 1960s and early 1970s that serious "ethical" investing was introduced. Among idealistic young (and not-so-young) opponents to US military involvement in Vietnam, it was felt that a "socially screened" investment vehicle could be established to separate arms makers from other companies.

The first such portfolios were designed for clients who wanted to avoid companies connected to the war effort. Organised protests against companies involved in military production were matched with new thinking on how to make investments without feeling compromised; existing unit trusts (called mutual funds in the US) were screened for financial return only.

A conjunction of events led to the creation of socially screened unit trusts that could be marketed to individuals as well as institutions, and these did not screen just for defence-related issues. These factors included:

- the rise of a strong consumer movement that studied the standards of product quality and production, including environmental protection and product safety;
- growing unrest in American cities, which prompted a new awareness of the social and infrastructural disintegration of disadvantaged communities and the need to reverse it;
- the women's movement, which spurred women to agitate for better treatment;
- and a rising environmental awareness, brought about in part by the first international Earth Day in 1970;
- finally — but not least — a heightened concern about rising repression under apartheid South Africa spurred many opponents of that system to seek to disinvest of any holding in companies that continued to operate in South Africa.

Creative financial professionals seized the opportunity to market their services to customise portfolios for investors who wanted to avoid "bad" companies and support "good" ones — making sure the "good" ones were also profitable. Smaller investors could eventually buy shares of unit trusts in which the companies were screened according to "ethical" standards.

A few funds got off to wobbly starts — and amid great scepticism — in the early 1970s. By the 1980s a number were performing very well and their popularity grew. In 1988, two 'ethical funds ranked among the top 10 in the US — out of 1 470 altogether!

SRI comes of age

Now fast forward to the 1990s: SRI has come of age. Baby-boomers, with many high earners among them, have made SRI an acceptable investing option. In 1994, the Social Investment Forum, a US-based umbrella organisation for social investment professionals, reported US$625 billion invested using some form of social screening including $25 billion in explicit socially-screened unit trusts. Trade union provident and pension funds, huge state municipal pension funds, religious funds and universities are among the institutional investors using social screens.

Nowadays, an array of socially responsible unit trusts is available to individual and institutional investors in the US, Canada, the United Kingdom and Australia.

The fund screens vary widely. Some funds focus on specific types of investment, such as the Green Century Fund and the New Alternatives Fund, which are environmental funds. Others make their choices based on a broader array of concerns.

In the UK, where investors can choose from about a dozen funds, the screening process can be quite detailed. The *Guide to EIRIS Research* (see chapter 8 for more information on EIRIS) describes more than 30 different screens that may be used in selecting companies for investment or avoidance. These range from such broad categories as community investment and environmental activity to such specific concerns as animal testing, whether a company sells alcohol products or pornographic materials, or, in the case of a food manufacturer operating farms, whether it treats the animals it maintains in a humane fashion.

Socially responsible investing in South Africa

South African investors currently have three funds available to them that use social screens. The first is the **Community Growth Fund** unit trust, launched in 1992 and managed by a trade union consortium. Its investors include huge trade union funds as well as individuals, who can deposit as little as R30 per month. CGF's social screening, which is conducted by Labour Research Service in Cape Town, emphasises workplace issues, but it also screens companies for their environmental records and social investment.

The CGF draws on 14 criteria, which are weighted on a base of 100 points. They are:

Jobs: 14 points
Industrial relations: 14 points
Conditions of employment: 13 points
Training: 7 points
Equal opportunities for women: 7 points
Health and safety: 6 points
Product: 5 points
Privatisation; 5 points
Profit retention: 5 points
Affirmative action: 5 points
Location: 4 points
Environment: 4 points
Worker participation: 4 points
Disclosure: 4 points
Political profile: 2 points
Social spending: 1 point

CGF has performed strongly since its founding. By mid-June 1994, two years after its launch, CGF reported returns of 45,6 percent for the year to June, outstripping the performance of the all-share index, making it one of the top three performers among SA's then 23 general equity funds. By then, Unity Incorporation, the union-controlled company which screens investments for the CGF, had approved 32 companies for investment and rejected 14.

In August 1994, CGF received its first infusion of foreign investment, when the US-based Calvert Group announced it would invest more than R3,6 million ($US 1 million) in the Fund.

As in the case of US socially screened funds, CGF has had impact. For instance, Berzack Brothers, a company that had been rejected in 1992 because of poor labour relations, was deemed an acceptable investment after the firm negotiated with union Mewusa to appoint workers to regional steering committees to implement workplace changes regarding affirmative action and training programmes.

But sometimes the choices are difficult; CGF approved Amalgamated Beverage Industries for investment despite a recent serious strike, because it pays above-average wages and has a generally good industrial relations record. Other new approvals in mid-1994 included the insurance firms African Life and Metropolitan Life because each had changed ownership to promote black economic empowerment.

FOR INFORMATION, contact Community Growth Management Company Limited at PO Box 4815, Cape Town 8000, tel. (021) 488-2911.

Futuregrowth, launched in 1994 by Southern Life, is a different type of socially responsible investment. It channels pension funds directly into what are known as economically targeted investments (ETIs) that directly meet the requirements of the RDP. It has two types of investments: an Income Fund and a Balanced Fund. A percentage of the Income Fund's cash deposits is held in FutureBank, a black-led bank whose principal shareholders are First National Bank and Fabcos.

Futuregrowth's holdings include CHIPS, a fixed-interest security which provides funds to enable the Independent Development Trust Finance Corporation to advance money to retail lenders for low-income housing loans; Electrification Participation Notes (EPNs), which are dedicated to the provision of pre-paid electricity meters in low-income households; and commercial property investments in low-income areas with high growth potential. The Balanced Fund has holdings in New South Africa Equity Investments, a firm which has just launched its first franchised operation, and in Nyanga Junction Shopping Centre, the first of its kind in the Western Cape township.

Toward the end of 1994 Futuregrowth reported assets of R200 million. Newcomers to Futuregrowth fund included Iscor, First National Bank, Eskom and several pension fund investments. Individuals may not invest in Futuregrowth.

FOR INFORMATION, contact Futuregrowth coordinator Michael Leeman at The Southern Life Association Limited, Great Westerford, Rondebosch 7700, tel. (021) 658-0461 or fax (021) 658-0347.

The **Southern Pure Specialist Fund** is a unit trust also sponsored by Southern Life. Much smaller than the other two, it is packaged as a "sin-free" fund that screens out companies that manufacture liquor or tobacco products; hotels that distribute liquor or sponsor casinos; wholesale and retail pork distributors; and interest-bearing instruments such as banks or insurance companies.

The Fund also avoids companies with poor environmental records. Its stringent screening criteria limits it to about 60 companies on the JSE, and its liquid assets are held with banks that practice interest-free banking, which include just the Islamic Bank in Johannesburg and the Albaraka Bank in Cape Town.

FOR INFORMATION, contact Shams Pather at tel. (021) 658-0911.

Community banking: Hands-on social investment to bring banking to the "unbankable"

At a time when many banks were scaling back operations, South Africa's new Community Bank (CBSA) was up and running in May 1994. The nation's first mutual bank, it aims to provide low-cost housing loans of up to R30 000 to clients whose monthly income is about R1 200; loans ranging from R3 000 to R6 000 for informal housing, and micro-enterprise loans. CBSA raised initial capitalisation of R2 billion from the Independent Development Trust, the Industrial Development Corporation and the Development Bank of Southern Africa.

The country's four largest banks have also helped out, by funding salaries, charging a low rent for office space and seconding executives to help get CBSA off the ground. And NGOs such as the Get Ahead Foundation, the National Stokvels Association of South Africa and the Group Housing Company have endorsed it.

How it works

Headquartered in Johannesburg, CBSA began opening branches in urban, high-density, low-income areas in different parts of the country, including Benoni, Athlone in Cape Town and downtown Johannesburg. Before a branch opens, CBSA liaison officers, preferably based in the community, run workshops to educate residents on the bank's services, often working through burial societies and stokvels. Each outlet is autonomous so that if one has problems, other branches are not affected.

The bank does *not* offer cheque accounts, which customers could, if they qualify, get from other banks. Over time, CBSA's network will be linked to ATMs so that clients can access cash.

As a mutual bank, CBSA is owned by its customers. Any customer must buy at least one R10 share in CBSA, and no matter how many shares he or she holds, each "owner" is entitled to one vote when major policy changes are proposed. Corporate investors may have the option of buying more voting shares, but these could be designated as a different class of share. But the bank will ensure that corporate owners won't overwhelm the general constituency.

A role for CSI
There are several roles that social investment can play to support community banks. First, a portion of CSI budgets may be invested in them, so that before money is designated for a project, it is already being used for development. Second, depositors may opt for lower-interest accounts, funnelling the extra interest into development projects. This is the model used by Chicago's South Shore Bank, which created lower-interest "development deposits" in which the balance is ploughed into low-income housing.

FOR INFORMATION on CBSA, call Nozipho Grootboom of the CBSA Foundation at (011) 332-8179 or 332-8131 or send a fax to (011) 332-8154.

Outlook for SRI in South Africa
At this writing, many of the socially screened unit trusts in the US had dropped their screens barring investing in companies with operations or licensing agreements in South Africa; some had begun researching prospects for direct investments. The Fund for a Free South Africa (FreeSA) was in the process of creating a loan fund to support black-owned small businesses. Many of these developments were still getting of the ground as this book was being prepared.

CHAPTER 8

Resources for further research

Research on corporate social responsibility, socially responsible investment and development is becoming a global process, at universities, non-governmental organisations and in some cases by research institutions associated with government.

The following list is a *sampling* of organisations and publications involved with research on CSI or the non-profit world.

In South Africa:

Business & Marketing Intelligence (BMI)
ITG House, 356 Rivonia Boulevard
Rivonia 2128
Phone: (011) 803-6412; Fax (011) 803-4676

BMI Issues Management publishes research reports on affirmative action and education, including *The Role of Business in Education and Training* (see below). The Issues Management division is branching into studies of the RDP and community involvement. A former BMI research unit run by Bets Nel, now called Corporate Services Research (CSR) has spun off as an independent entity, but operates at BMI premises. Nel conducts a 'Corporate Care Check' that monitors CSI programmes at certain companies. Her research is underwritten by corporations to whom the information is distributed. It is not available to non-subscribers.

Centre for Policy Studies (CPS)
PO Box 16488
Doornfontein 2028
Phone: (011) 402-4308; Fax: (011) 402-7755

CPS's research covers a wide spectrum of issues which occasionally include business and society. Two 1989 CPS publications give a valuable perspective on the status of CSI and the voluntary sector prior to the changes that started on 2 February 1990. These are *The Future of the Nonprofit Voluntary Sector in South Africa* by Robin Lee and Fran Buntman (Research Report, No 5, April 1989) and *The Business Sector and Policy Change: An Empirical Study: 1985-1988* by Robin Lee (Research Report No 6, October 1989).

CSI Letter
PO Box 91070
Auckland Park 2006
Phone: (011) 482-3580; Fax: (011) 482-3485

CSI Letter is a bi-monthly newsletter on corporate social investment in South Africa and is published by *The Innes Labour Brief*. It provides an overview of new developments in CSI and, through features written in-house and by outside contributors, examines strategies to implement effective CSI, the interaction between companies and their employees (with considerable attention to the role of trade unions), and the impact of socially responsible investments on corporate behaviour; it also discusses new trends in CSI programming.

Development Contact Network (DCN)
50 Umbilo Road
Durban 4001
Phone: (031) 305-5452; Fax: (031) 305-9721

DCN began as the Education Contact Network, a spin-off of the Urban Foundation's Durban office, as a way to inform educational organisations of possible funders. ECN's coordinator, Alan Brews, feeling ECN was encouraging a one-way, paternalistic process, came up with a new approach to offer courses that would train development professionals in managing their organisations, including doing their own fundraising. This process helps the organisations become self-sufficient. DCN publishes a *Development Diary* which not only updates subscribers on courses and conferences but also provides information on development projects in which groups can collaborate. It focuses on Natal, and although courses had previously all been held at DCN's Durban offices, the organisation now runs 'train-the-trainer' courses so that its methods can be exported to rural areas. DCN is joining a networking initiative with PRODDER (see p206) to develop a national database on NGOs.

Development Resources Centre (DRC)
PO Box 6079
Johannesburg 2000
Phone: (011) 838-7504; Fax: (011) 838-6310

DRC, which opened in 1992, is South Africa's first national information and training resource centre for NGOs and corporate donors. It has a development library available to users at no charge, runs an array of training courses, and coordinated the 18-month "Enabling Study on NGOs" which brought together legal, financial and development experts to analyse the potential impact of new legislative, economic, taxation and other issues confronting NGOs in the new environment, and to make recommendations to facilitate the functioning of NGOs.

Institute for Personnel Management (IPM)
PO Box 31390
Braamfontein 2017
Phone: (011) 642-7263; Fax: (011) 642-3526

IPM principally addresses human resources concerns in South Africa, and offers courses and conferences to promote new thinking and skills in this field. However, it recognises the linkages with CSI in some of its programmes and publications. Articles on CSI appear regularly in its bi-monthly magazine, *People Dynamics*.

Labour Research Service (LRS)
PO Box 376
Salt River 7927
Phone: (021) 471-677/8; Fax: (021) 479-244

Among its many projects to empower the trade union movement, LRS designed the social screening format for companies in the Community Growth Fund (CGF) portfolio and conducts the research to help determine which companies should be included in or excluded from investment (see Chapter 7). It also publishes a magazine, *Trustee Digest*, which examines issues of concern to the trustees of union pension and provident funds.

National Business Initiative (NBI)
PO Box 294
Auckland Park 2006
Phone: (011) 482-5100; Fax: (011) 482-5507

NBI is the successor organisation to the Consultative Business
Movement (CBM), which was formed in 1988 as the result of a
long consultation process between 40 senior business leaders and
40 community leaders. During its first year of activities, it made a
point of consulting groups across the political spectrum, from the
Afrikaner Volksfront to the PAC. It aims, through conferences and
publications, to promote a positive role for business and the development of a non-racial democracy, and to advocate for social
progress within South Africa in such areas as education, housing,
welfare, health and job creation. It also seeks to provide a positive
image of South Africa internationally on behalf of business. CBM's
two recent books, *Managing Change* (1993) and *Building a
Winning Nation* (1994), both published by Ravan Press, are discussed elsewhere in this section. NBI was formed through a merg-
er of CBM's principals and some leaders at the Urban Foundation,
a private sector initiative that operated from 1976 to 1994.

Programme for Development Research (PRODDER)
PO Box 32410
Braamfontein 2017
Phone: (011) 339-4451; Fax: (011) 403-2353

The Programme for Development Research (PRODDER) was
established in 1987 by the Human Sciences Research Council
(HSRC) as a medium to disseminate information on Southern
African development issues and organisations. It publishes an
annual *Southern African Development Directory* and a quarterly
newsletter. In 1994 it introduced a series of development forums
that aim at capacity-building for NGO staff members. The
Directory lists NGOs throughout Southern African, including
Angola, Botswana, Lesotho, Malawi, Mauritius, Mozambique,
Namibia, South Africa, Swaziland, Tanzania, Zambia and
Zimbabwe. It also sources information on the Preferential Trade
Area of East and Southern Africa, and the Southern African
Customs Union and the African Development Bank. PRODDER is
taking a leading role in overseeing the development of a compre-
hensive database on southern African NGOs. The PRODDER

newsletter is free and currently has about 10 000 subscribers world-wide, including government departments, donors, researchers, development agencies and others involved in Southern African development.

SANGONeT
(South African NGO Network)
PO Box 31
Johannesburg 2000
Phone: (011) 838-6943/4; Fax: (011) 838-6310
E-MAIL: SN0004@CONNECTINC. COM

SANGONeT, which was launched by the US-based WorkNet and the Development Resources Centre (see p205) is a not-for-gain electronic mail and information service which links subscribers to each other and to users of other networks worldwide. It is a member of the Association for Progressive Communication and the Internet, two international groups. Subscription fees are divided into three categories: CBO rate (for community-based non-profit organisations with local community leadership); the NGO rate (for non-profits with annual budgets of up to R100 million); and the "pay your own way" rate for for-profit, para-government and governmental organisations. It provides information on conferences, helps organisations write fundraising proposals and includes information on new publications and policy debates. At this writing SANGONeT reported 500 members.

South African Grantmakers' Association (SAGA)
Interim contact address:
Hugh McLean, Treasurer
Liberty Life Foundation
PO Box 10499
Johannesburg 2000
Phone: (011) 408-3298; Fax: (011) 408-3998

Launched in August 1994, SAGA aims to bring together corporate and other donors to provide a self-help support network and give a unified voice to donors in South Africa's redevelopment efforts. It endeavours to promote projects on which donors might collaborate and provide information on trends and changes in CSI. In response to criticism of its first proposal plans to charge a membership fee based on the size of donations budgets, new donor-members will be charged the same fee (although a lower fee is being considered for very small companies). Other donor-members include the Kagiso Trust, the Ford Foundation, the Kellogg Foundation and the Charles Stewart Mott Foundation. The Ford and Mott Foundations have made grants to SAGA. A new director, Elaine Davie, was named in May 1995. Davie is the founder of an educare NGO called Small Beginnings.

The Mail & Guardian
Reg Rumney, Business Editor
PO Box 32362
Braamfontein 2017
Phone: (011) 403-7111; Fax: (011) 403-1025

Since 1991, *M&G* has sponsored a special annual supplement on 'Investing in the Future', which explores CSI from the corporate, trade union and community viewpoints. It highlights a few of South Africa's 'Most Caring Companies' with an awards programme. Winners have included AECI (1991), Pick 'n Pay (1992) and The Premier Group (1993), with several runners-up also identified each year. The 1994 competition changed its focus to honour companies that supported the most original projects. Winners were The Southern Life Foundation (for being one of the first supporters of the Triple Trust Organisation) and Toyota (for Toyota Teach). Pick 'n Pay won an award for the most thorough social reporting.

In the United Kingdom and Europe:

Directory of Social Change (DSC)
Radius Works
Back Lane, London NW3 1HL, UK

DSC has published a number of studies of European philanthropy. Among these are:
1. *Company giving in Europe*, edited by Brian Dabson, 1991. This book examines global trends in philanthropy and then profiles one to three CSI programmes by major companies in Belgium, Denmark, France, Germany, Greece, Ireland, Italy, The Netherlands, Portugal, Spain and the United Kingdom, as well as several "Pan-European" companies.
2. *Promoting Corporate Community Investment in Europe: A directory of intermediary and partnership organisations in the*

European Community, edited by John Griffiths, 1993. This book discusses the role of the socially responsible corporation within the European Community and then explores philanthropy trends and styles in Belgium, Denmark, France, Germany, Greece, Ireland, Italy, Luxembourg, The Netherlands, Portugal, Spain and the United Kingdom as well as international organisations. For each country it identifies the principal intermediary organisations and information agencies that serve as "go-betweens" between corporations and NGOs.
3. *Transnational Giving: An introduction to the corporate citizenship activity of international companies operating in Europe,* by David Logan, 1993. This profiles the CSI programmes run by global companies American Express, Canon, Ciba-Geigy, Daimler-Benz, Elf Aquitaine, IBM, Olivetti and Royal Dutch Shell, as well as three international European firms, Allied Dunbar, NV Bekaert and Sanofi. The book was published for Corporate Community Investment in Europe (CCIE), a business committee of the European Foundation Centre (see p210).

Ethical Investment Research Service (EIRIS)
504 Bondway Business Centre
71 Bondway
London SW8 1SQ, UK
Phone: (071) 735-1351; Fax: (071) 735-5323

Formed in 1983, EIRIS was the first organisation in Europe to focus on corporate-social research. Its categories include external CSI concerns, such as community investment, human rights, military involvement and the environment as well as such workplace issues as equal opportunities, health and safety and training and education, thus defining CSI in a much broader way. It has played an influential role in helping investors wanting to make socially responsible decisions by conducting research on the social records of British and other European companies. It publishes a quarterly newsletter, *The Ethical Investor,* and has produced a number of focused studies, including one in 1988 on South African Employment Conditions.

European Foundation Centre (EFC)
51, Rue de la Concorde
B-1050 Brussels, BELGIUM
Phone: 32-2-512-8938; Fax: 32-2-512-3265

One of EFC's recent publications is an EFC Occasional Paper (February 1994): *Corporate Citizenship in the New Europe: A report on the Corporate Citizenship Europe Business Committee Conference, Barcelona, Spain, October 7-8, 1993*. This examines the progress of corporate citizenship programmes by Western companies that have started new operations in Eastern Europe.

New Consumer
52 Elswick Road
Newcastle upon Tyne NE4 6JH, UK
Phone: (091) 272-1148

New Consumer is a public interest research organisation whose principal goals are to reinforce the public's awareness of consumers' clout to influence business conduct. One of its major publications is *Changing Corporate Values: A guide to Social and Environmental Policy and Practice in Britain's top companies* (London: Kogan Page, 1991). The book, by New Consumer staffers Richard Adams, Jane Carruthers and Sean Hamil, explores the convergence of consumer and corporate values in such areas as employment issues (including wages and working conditions, equal opportunities), social investment, foreign operations and environmental stewardship, and then profiles the social records of 129 consumer firms. Since 1993 New Consumer has been engaged in a cooperative project with the Council on Economic Priorities to explore the social records of major transnational companies.

In the United States:

Africa Fund/American Committee on Africa
17 John Street
New York, New York 10038, USA
Phone: (212) 962-1210

For many years the Africa Fund and its allied group American Committee on Africa played an important role in publicising the struggle for democracy in South Africa through campaigns, publications and fundraising efforts to support self-help projects. Since the 1994 election, the organisation has served as a liaison between South African capacity-building organisations and US groups wanting to provide support, and is broadening its work in the continent.

Business for Social Responsibility (BSR)
1030 15th Street, NW, suite 1010
Washington, DC 20005, USA
Phone: (202) 842-5400; Fax: (202) 842-3135

BSR was founded in 1992 by a charter group of 54 companies attempting to speak with a unified voice in promoting a positive ethic of corporate social behaviour. It had over 800 members by mid-1994 and is now launching regional and local chapters. Since 1993, BSR sponsors an annual national conference focusing on its four target areas of concern to business: 1) the workplace, 2) the marketplace, 3) the community, and 4) sustainable development. Membership fees are on a sliding scale based on annual corporate revenues, and special memberships are available to national and regional non-profit organisations and to individual non-voting members.

The Conference Board
845 Third Avenue
New York, New York 10022, USA
Phone: (212) 759-0900; Fax: (212) 980-7014

The Conference Board, established in 1916, is a global business research and networking organisation which sponsors forums and research to promote new ideas that have an impact on business policy and practices. It sponsors seminars and conferences worldwide and produces research on business and society; human resources; corporate governance; and economic trends. It also runs a Total Quality Management centre and an environmental management centre. Reports in the business and society area for 1994 cover such topics as the impact of corporate support for volunteerism and the extent of social investment by foreign companies in the US. Its two current research themes in this area are "Business and Society 2000", and "Global Corporate Stewardship". (The author of the present study joined The Conference Board as a senior research associate in the Business and Society unit in September 1994.)

Corporate Citizen
2727 Fairview Avenue East
Seattle, Washington 98102, USA
Phone: (206) 329-0422; Fax: (206) 325-1382

Corporate Citizen is a think-tank/research organisation that monitors the social responsibility of international companies and is conducting a study to measure corporate citizenship. Founder-president Craig Smith, who for many years published a newsletter on corporate philanthropy, is the author of an article entitled 'The New Corporate Philanthropy' (*Harvard Business Review*, May-June 1994) which explores how companies support movements for social change while also advancing their business goals.

Council on Economic Priorities (CEP)
30 Irving Place
New York, New York 10003, USA
Phone: (212) 420-1133; Fax: (212) 420-0988

CEP was formed in 1968 as a not-for-profit public interest research organisation specialising in evaluating the policies and practices of US corporations and issues affecting national security. It publishes monthly research reports and has produced numerous books examining CSR and corporate stewardship in industries such as banking, nuclear energy, the paper industry and defence contracting.

Foundation Center
79 Fifth Avenue
New York, New York 10003-3076, USA
Phone: (212) 620-4230; Fax: (212) 807-3677

The Foundation Center publishes a series of directories on grantmaking, including funding guides on health, higher education, religions, women's issues and AIDS, and also sponsors a comprehensive library of newsletters, books and reports — in print and on microfilm — of information for institutional and individual grantmakers and grantseekers. Its library contains many works that track trends in international philanthropy. The Center has satellite libraries in other major US cities.

Fund for a Free South Africa (FreeSA)
729 Boylston Street
Boston, Massachusetts 02116, USA
Phone: (617) 267-8333; Fax: (617) 267-2585

FreeSA was formed in 1986 by South African exiles in the US to provide financial and technical support to development, educational and human rights programmes that promote literacy and self-sufficiency in disadvantaged communities. In addition to its grants programme, it runs a social investment programme called Shared Interest, launched in 1992, which offers loans that support black-owned small and medium-sized businesses. At this writing FreeSA was exploring the creation of a workplace-giving programme at South African companies. FreeSA has a satellite office in Johannesburg.

Interfaith Centre on Corporate Responsibility (ICCR)
475 Riverside Drive, room 566
New York, New York 10115-0050, USA
Phone: (212) 870-2936

Founded in 1971, ICCR is a membership organisation of some 275 Protestant and Roman Catholic orders, denominations, agencies, dioceses, health care corporations and pension funds which take the idea of responsible stewardship into the corporate arena. Using their clout as institutional shareholders, they challenge the power of multinational corporations to do what they want with impunity, with a particular focus on ensuring human rights, economic justice, environmental stewardship and workplace equity. Specific targets have included South Africa, Northern Ireland, international health (with special attention to the marketing of tobacco products to young people), infant formula sales, militarism and capital flight. ICCR's particular "weapon" is the shareholder resolution, which seeks to influence corporate policy.

International Society for Third Sector Research (ISTR)
The Johns Hopkins University
Shriver Hall
Baltimore, MD 21218-2689, USA
Phone: (410) 516-4678; Fax: (410) 516-8233

ISTR is a new organisation that brings together researchers and practitioners involved in voluntary and non-profit organisations.

Members come from over 70 countries worldwide. ISTR publishes a journal called *Voluntas* and sponsored its first international conference in Pecs, Hungary, in July 1994. Its membership newsletter, *Inside ISTR*, provides valuable information on new articles and books, lists conferences worldwide and helps link up affinity groups in such areas as NGOs and development and the politics of nonprofit sector research.

Investor Responsibility Research Centre (IRRC)
1350 Connecticut Avenue, NW, suite 700
Washington, DC 20036, USA
Phone: (202) 833-0700

Founded in 1972, IRRC monitors shareholder resolutions on key social issues of concern to institutional investors; screens investment portfolios for institutional investment clients; and provides regular news updates on the role institutional investors may play in influencing corporate social behaviour. It has done special reporting in South Africa for many years and in 1994 formed a partnership with McGregor's On-Line Services to provide more direct information on investment developments in South Africa for local and US clients. It is supported principally by annual membership/ subscription fees.

Mandel Centre for Non-Profit Organisations, Case Western Reserve University
Case Western Reserve University
10900 Euclid Avenue
Cleveland, OH 44106-7164, USA
Phone: (216) 368-1687; Fax: (216) 368-8592

The Mandel Centre runs an interdisciplinary programme which links the university's law school, its Weatherhead School of Management and the Mandel School of Applied Social Sciences. Its programmes include a Masters of Non-profit Organisations degree and a Certificate in Non-profit Management, as well as executive workshops and lectures and conferences and research; it publishes a newsletter called *Non-profit Notes*.

Non-Profit Sector Research Fund, Aspen Institute
1333 New Hampshire Avenue, NW, suite 1070
Washington, DC 20036, USA
Phone: (202) 736-5800; Fax: (202) 467-0790

This fund was formed in 1991 by a consortium of donors to support research on the non-profit sector. It funds doctoral research and some institutional research. Its areas of interest are democracy; role of the non-profit sector; advocacy; philanthropy; governance; public accountability; financial resources; the non-profit sector workforce; and international dimensions.

Prince of Wales Business Leaders Forum (PWBLF)
5 Cleveland Place
St. James's, London SW1 6JJ
United Kingdom
Phone: (071) 321-6464; Fax: (071) 321-6480

PWBLF is a consortium of multinational companies who advocate for better business practices in developing countries. In particular, it supports development partnerships that will ultimately strengthen local economies through skills-building initiatives. It is an outgrowth of the group Business in the Community.

Programme on Non-Profit Organizations (PONPO)
Yale University
PO Box 208253
New Haven, Connecticut 06520-8253, USA

Formed in 1977, PONPO sponsors interdisciplinary research on non-profit organisations, ranging from the interaction between trade unions and foundations and the role of donors and NGOs in developing countries. Its *Research Reports* contains valuable information on international research, but despite its breadth, one key area appears to be missing among its conferences and sponsored research: the interaction between business and non-profits.

South African Information Exchange (SAIE)
Institute of International Education
809 United Nations Plaza
New York, New York 10017-3580, USA
Phone: (212) 984-5364; Fax: (212)984-5452

SAIE produces regular directories of funders, programmes and
NGOs in South Africa and elsewhere whose work is South Africa-
related, as well as working papers on such topics as the role of
voluntary organisations in emerging democracies and discussion
forum presentations. Topics from 1993-94 include The US
Independent Sector as it relates to South African Initiatives; the
Donor Community in South Africa and Foreign Assistance to South
Africa. SAIE's data are also available on SANGONeT in South
Africa.

**Association for Research in the Voluntary and Community
Sector** (ARVAC)
Unit 29, Wivenhoe Business Centre
Brook Street
Wivenhoe, Essex CO7 9DP, UK
Phone/Fax: (0206) 824281

Established in 1978, ARVAC brings together academic researchers
and members of the voluntary and parastatal sectors to share information on policy-making and practice. It publishes a quarterly bulletin and sponsors conferences and seminars for researchers, practitioners, policy-makers and funders. It offers training in carrying
out research, both for grassroots community researchers and trained
professionals, and has a database of over 2 500 listings.

Social Investment Forum (SIF)
PO Box 57216
Washington, DC 20037, USA
Phone: (202) 833-5522; Fax: (202) 331-8166

SIF is the umbrella association for individuals and organisations
engaged directly or indirectly (as research or advocacy groups) in
socially responsible investing. It publishes a bi-monthly newsletter,
The Forum, and has regional chapters.

BOOKS AND NEWSLETTERS:

In South Africa
CSI reporting in South Africa has been fairly limited, but the following list contains a few key local examples as well as publications from elsewhere.

■ *The Role of Business in Education and Training in South Africa in the 1990s: A CSI perspective*, by Jonathan Harrod, Vanessa Rockey and Karen Molin (BMI, 1994). Researched and developed by the Issues Management division of BMI (see p203), this study provides a detailed breakdown of the interaction between companies and NGOs, the types of education programmes that are funded, the identities of the key players among the NGO and CBO education service providers, and how funds are allocated. It recommends how donors can get the most out of their CSI in education and includes a listing of companies considered to be most successful in education. In order, they are Anglo American, Liberty Life, Shell, Eskom, Nedcor, Engen, First National Bank, South African Breweries, Gencor and British Petroleum (BP).

■ *Managing Change: A guide to the role of business in transition* and *Building a Winning Nation: Companies and the RDP,* compiled by the Consultative Business Movement National Team (Johannesburg: Ravan Press, 1993 and 1994 respectively). These two short books provide a concise examination of the many ways business can contribute to South Africa's redevelopment process. *Managing Change* was the result of the first phase of the CBM's project focusing on the Role of Business in Transition (RoBiT), and offers practical strategies for business to cope during the transition. It evolved out of five working sessions held in 1992 with more than 200 business leaders nationwide. The book argues for business to become proactively involved as a key stakeholder in South Africa's future to help stem instability, poverty, conflict and uncertainty in the years ahead. Several case studies illustrate how companies such as Eskom, Nampak, PG Bison and Premier devised creative approaches to internal and community social investment to help spur economic growth. *Building a Winning Nation* expands on working papers developed in 1994 by task forces of leaders in business, academia and the trade union movement which looked at five areas: (1) private sector funding for the RDP; (2) global competitiveness; (3) human resource development; (4) technological advancement , and (5) support for small enterprise. In each book CSI is cited for its role in promoting democracy and the efforts to establish economic equity both as financing mechanisms and through programming. Appendices in each describe the networks involved in CBM.

■ *Money that Matters: An introduction to fundraising in South Africa,* by David Cuthbert (Pretoria: J P van der Walt, 1992). This book, the first of its kind in South Africa, focuses on the other side of money: how to get it. Its target readers are NGOs, churches, schools, boards, welfare organisations and other groups competing for funds from a shrinking pool of donors. It provides a brief history of the local fundraising scene and background on fundraising legislation, and provides guidelines for preparing a fundraising plan and doing the research to identify and approach prospective donors. It also looks at giving strategies (deferred giving, media promotion, etc.), how to use media and volunteer support, and then, when the money arrives, how to say thanks. The last chapter explores accountability, economic restrictions and taxation policy. An independent Johannesburg-based consultant, Cuthbert, is one of South Africa's experts in the field; he is a founder-member of the Southern African Institute of Fundraising, vice-president of the World Fundraising Council and the first South African to hold the title of Certified Fundraising Executive, awarded by the US-based National Society of Fundraising Executives. A new edition was planned for late 1994.

■ *The Southern African Development Directory, 1994 Edition,* edited by David Barnard (Braamfontein: Programme for Development Research, Human Sciences Research Council, 1994). This book contains information on hundreds of NGOs throughout Southern Africa (see citation for PRODDER p206).

Outside South Africa

■ *Beyond the Bottom Line: Putting social responsibility to work for your business and the world,* by Joel Makower and Business for Social Responsibility (New York: Simon & Schuster, 1994). Makower examines what he calls a trend by companies which have found that proactive, pro-employee practices, such as extensive family benefits and environmental policies that exceed minimum regulations are actually good for business. He explores environmental stewardship, worker welfare, human rights and corporate globalisation, and the relationship between being a "good" company and doing well — i.e., making money — and gives case studies on a broad range of companies of various sizes, types and profiles that have chosen to carve reputations for social responsibility.

■ *Chronicle of Philanthropy,* 1255 23rd Street, NW, Washington, DC 20037, USA, Phone: (202) 466-1200: A bi-weekly newsletter, it provides comprehensive coverage of international philanthropy trends, including updates of grants by foundations and companies; discussions of new ideas and resources in the field; new developments in the philanthropy world; listings of new publications, studies and awards; and reports on how well-selected foundations have complied with regulations on disclosure and record-keeping. It also contains an extensive listing of jobs in the field.

■ *Corporate Citizenship in Australia,* by Max Dumais and Carol Cohn (Tokyo: Sasakawa Peace Foundation, 1993). This book contains 10 case studies of companies with operations in Australia, divided by themes. For instance, it examines how the Mazda Foundation has focused on cultural exchanges, while the British and US firms The Body Shop and Esprit have concentrated on youth homelessness.

■ *Corporate Citizenship in Thailand and the Philippines,* by Sinfah Tunsarawuth and Jose Jesus F Ignacio (Tokyo: Sasakawa Peace Foundation, 1991). This book contains five case studies each of corporate/community projects in Thailand and the Philippines. In Thailand, for example, Volvo set up a local company to help give business skills as well as small loans to farmers as a way of promoting self-reliance. In the Philippines the Shell Foundation supported an agricultural skills training project which formed linkages with other companies.

■ *Corporate Giving Watch,* The Taft Group, 835 Penobscot Building, Detroit, Michigan 48226, USA: This monthly newsletter targets non-profit organisations seeking corporate funding. It includes occasional lengthy profiles of corporate philanthropy programmes, drawing on publicly available tax returns, annual reports and other published information, and examines the spending programmes, a corporate analysis, who to contact, funding priorities and previous recipients, the philosophy of giving, how decisions are made as well as restrictions.

■ *Corporate Philanthropy Report,* Capitol Publications, 1101 King Street, suite 444, Alexandria, VA 22314, USA, Phone: (703) 683-4100; Fax: (703) 739-6517: A 10-page monthly newsletter (except September and January), it includes interviews with leaders in the corporate philanthropy area (the July 1994 interview was with Stanley Litow, the new head of IBM's corporate support programme and president of the IBM International Foundation).

■ *Corporate Responsibility,* by Tom Cannon (London: Pitman Publishing, 1992, 267 pp.). Despite its dry title, this book — which was probably written as a business school text — offers an animated discussion on the topic of corporate responsibility (CR), which Cannon defines to apply to every aspect of how a company functions (see chapter 1 of this book), including general business ethics; governance and compliance; the environment as it pertains to workers and communities; and the "economically and socially disadvantaged", both in and beyond the workplace. An overriding theme is the need for transparency: companies must provide complete information on how they work and allow outsiders to audit and critique them. *Corporate Responsibility* is full of charts and footnotes. But it is also often ironic and witty. Cannon peppers his text with references from Cicero, Chaucer, Swift and De Tocqueville, as well as the movies *Modern Times,* *Wall Street* and *Other People's Money.* The book can be obtained from Pitman Publishing, 128 Long Acre, London WC2E 9AN.

■ *Directory of Foundation and Corporate Members of the European Foundation Centre* (1993/94 edition). This book contains 85 thorough profiles of foundations and corporate funders active in Europe and intercontinentally. Each profile lists trustees, goals, local programmes and how to make contact. It received broad support from British, French, US and other major funders.

■ *Directory of International Corporate Giving in America and Abroad* (Detroit: The Taft Group, 1994). This book is divided into two sections and contains overviews of the corporate-giving programmes of 365 companies. The first section examines foreign-owned companies with US operations and summarises their contribution programmes, the contact people at each one, the type of support they give, a description of their programmes, a sampling of typical recipients, and the names of the operating companies owned by the parent company. The second section examines the CSI programmes of 160 US companies with international programmes.

■ *Inside Japanese Support: Descriptive profiles and other information on Japanese corporate giving and foundation giving programmes*, a co-publication of The Taft Group and the Foundation Library Centre of Japan. This book includes an essay on the history of Japanese philanthropy, trends during the 1960s and 1970s, and more recent developments.

■ *International Foundation Directory, Sixth Edition* (London: Europa Publications, 1994). A directory with detailed information on more than 1 200 trusts, foundations and grantmakers in 70 countries from Albania to Fiji and Tanzania and Zimbabwe. It includes a good history of foundations in the UK, continental Europe and the US, and also has information on exchange rates and currencies. Its section on South Africa does not include any corporate donors.

■ *It's Good Business*, by Robert C. Solomon and Kristine Hanson (New York: New York Perennial Library, 1986). Targeting corporate executives and managers, this book examines how ethics improves performance, the role of corporate culture and a section on why social responsibility is good business.

■ *Japanese Corporate Citizenship in the United Kingdom* (Tonbridge: Charities Aid Foundation, 1991). This examines Japanese CSI in the UK, including support for lectureships, cultural organisations and festivals.

■ *Japanese Corporate Philanthopy*, by Nancy London (Oxford: Oxford University Press, 1991). This book examines the development of the non-profit system in Japan, forming a foundation, taxation and the philanthropic process.

■ *Ju$t Rewards: The case for ethical reform in business*, by David Olive (Toronto: Key Porter Books, 1987). This book surveys ethical business issues from a Canadian perspective although it also cites US examples. It includes case studies of Canadian robber barons and bankers who created their own law in attaining power and wealth, and how they were stopped. It also examines how good companies have created codes of conduct. Canada's Royal Bank distributes copies of its Code of Conduct Principles of Ethical Behaviour to all employees, who are encouraged to discuss it at their performance appraisal interview. Other companies cited include Johnson & Johnson, whose "Our Credo" was first drafted in the 1940s and is posted in its offices worldwide, and J C Penney Company, which gives wallet-sized cards bearing "The Penney Idea" to all employees. It contains seven objectives, the last of which ends with the question: 'Does it square with what is right and just?' The book also examines the impact of university activism on corporate behaviour; whistleblowers and activists; and the rise of socially responsible investing. It contains an ample appendix and bibliography.

■ *Tercer Sector,* (Serrano 2297, Buenos Aires (1425), Argentina): *Tercer Sector* is a new newsletter published by the Fundacion Del Viso which is dedicated to reporting on development issues through South America, including the problems faced by NGOs where foundation support is minimal. Its May 1994 issue describes the first private foundation set up by one of Cuba's leading singers to support cultural development. The two issues that had been published when this book went to press did not mention business inputs in local development, but the newsletter in format and content seems to be modelled on the *Chronicle of Philanthropy.* Its principal value to South Africans (who can read Spanish) is its animated approach to debates similar to those currently being waged in the NGO community in South Africa but for which there is no publication in which to air them.